MW01227261

HOLLYWOOD
PINAFORE Or
The Lad Who Loved A Salary

Music by
SIR ARTHUR SULLIVAN

Book and Lyrics Revised by
GEORGE S. KAUFMAN
(With deepest apologies to W. S. Gilbert)

★

★

DRAMATISTS
PLAY SERVICE
INC.

HOLLYWOOD PINAFORE Or The Lad Who Loved A Salary
Copyright © 1999, Anne Kaufman Schneider
ALL RIGHTS RESERVED

SPECIAL NOTE

Anyone receiving permission to produce HOLLYWOOD PINAFORE Or The Lad Who Loved A Salary is required (1) to give credit to the Authors as sole and exclusive Authors of the Play on the title page of all programs distributed in connection with performances of the Play and in all instances in which the title of the Play appears for purposes of advertising, publicizing or otherwise exploiting the Play and/or a production thereof. The name of the Authors must appear on separate lines, in which no other names appears, immediately beneath the title and in size of type equal to 50% of the largest, most prominent letter used for the title of the Play. No person, firm or entity may receive credit larger or more prominent than that accorded the Authors; and (2) to give the following acknowledgment on the title page of all programs distributed in connection with performances of the Play.

Book and lyrics by George S. Kaufman
Music by Sir Arthur Sullivan

HOLLYWOOD PINAFORE Or The Lad Who Loved A Salary was produced by Theater Ten Ten (Lynn Marie Macy and Judith Jarosz, Artistic Directors) in New York City on May 1, 1997. It was directed by David Fuller; the musical director was Ned Levy; the set design was by John Scheffler; the costume design was by Melanie Schmidt; the lighting design was by Michael P. Hairston; the assistant musical director was John Canary; the choreographer was Hal Simons; and the stage manager was Eileen Merle. The cast was as follows:

BEVERLY WILTSHIRE, a star ....Amy Barker

MAXIE FACTOR, makeup artist ....Amy Baxter

GLORIA MUNDI, a star ....Gillian Burke

CHIP, clapboard operator ....Louis Butelli

JOSEPH RUTTENBERG, cinematographer..James Cole

FIFI ZANUCK, actress..Laura Lindsay Cole

HANSEN McCORMICK, actor...Mark W. Hardin

BOB BECKET, publicist...Greg Horton

JOSEPH PORTER, head of the studio ....Nathan Hull

BRENDA BLOSSOM, Academy Award winner...............Judith Jarosz

MELBA STANWYCK, wardrobe mistress ....Stacie Kellie

MIKE CORCORAN, director ....David Kroll

BERNICE GREASEHEIMER, secretary ....Lorinda Lisitza

REMI MARTIN, actor ....Ron Lopez

HEBE, secretary to Joseph Porter........................Melissa Jane Martin

DUKE COVERL, head doorman ....Robert Armstrong Martin

MISS PEGGY, child star ....Stephanie Pakowitz

RALPH RACKSTRAW, writer ....Douglas Purcell

DICK LIVE-EYE, agent ....Christopher Sutton

RUBY SLIPPERS, secretary...Lisa Yeager

LOUHEDDA HOPSONS, gossip columnist................Cristiane Young

HOLLYWOOD PINAFORE Or The Lad Who Loved A Salary was produced by Max Gordon in association with Meyer Davis at the Alvin Theater, in New York City, in July, 1945. It was directed by George S. Kaufman; the set and lighting designs were by Jo Mielziner; the costume design was by Kathryn Kuhn and Mary Percy Schenck; the ballet was by Antony Tudor; and the production supervisor was Arnold Saint Subber. The cast was as follows:

JOSEPH W. PORTER, head of Pinafore Pictures............................Victor Moore

MIKE CORCORAN, a director ....George Rasely

RALPH RACKSTRAW, a writer..Gilbert Russell

DICK LIVE-EYE, an agent...William Gaxton

BRENDA BLOSSOM, a star ....Annamary Dicky

LOUHEDDA HOPSONS, a columnist..Shirley Booth

BOB BECKETT, a press agent...Russ Brown

MISS HEBE, Mr. Porter's Secretary ....Mary Wickes

MISS GLORIA MUNDI...Diana Corday

MISS BEVERLY WILSHIRE..Pamela Randell

LITTLE MISS PEGGY ....Ella Mayer

DOORMAN..Dan De Paolo

SECRETARIES ....Eleanor Prentiss, Durcilla Strain

GUARD...Ernest Taylor

4

MUSICAL NUMBERS

ACT ONE

1. WE ARE SIMPLE MOVIE FOLK — Company
2. I'M CALLED LITTLE BUTTER-UP — Louhedda and Company
3. WHEN AN AGENT'S NOT ENGAGED IN HIS EMPLOYMENT — Dick and Company
4. WHEREVER I ROAM / A MAIDEN OFTEN SEEN — Ralph and Company
5. I'M A BIG DIRECTOR AT PINAFORE — Corcoran
6. MIKE, WHAT'S THE NEWS (Recitative) — Louhedda and Corcoran
7. HERE ON THE LOT — Brenda
8. JOE PORTER'S CAR IS SEEN — Company
9. I AM THE MONARCH OF THE JOINT — Porter, Hebe and Women
10. WHEN I WAS A LAD — Porter and Chorus
11. A WRITER FILLS THE LOWEST NICHE — Ralph, Bob, Doorman and Writers
12. NEVER MIND THE WHY AND WHEREFORE — Dick, Secretaries and Company
13. REFRAIN AUDACIOUS SCRIBE — Brenda and Ralph
14. CAN I SURVIVE THIS — Ralph, Dick, Brenda and Company
15. A WRITER FILLS THE LOWEST NICHE (Act One Finale) — Company

ACT TWO

1. FAIR MOON — Corcoran
2. HOLLYWOOD'S A FUNNY PLACE — Louhedda and Porter
3. TO GO UPON THE STAGE — Brenda
4. HE IS A MOVIE MAN — Porter, Dick, Bob, Corcoran, Ralph, and Hebe
5. JOE PORTER, I'VE IMPORTANT INFORMATION — Dick and Porter
6. CAREFULLY ON TIPTOE STEALING — Brenda, Women, Ralph, Writers, Dick, Corcoran, Hebe and Porter
7. FAREWELL MY OWN — Ralph, Brenda, Porter, Dick, Louhedda, Hebe Bob and Company
8. THE TOWN I NOW MUST SHAKE — Louhedda and Company
9. WE ARE SIMPLE MOVIE FOLK (Finale) — Company

THE CHARACTERS

JOSEPH W. PORTER, head of Pinafore Pictures

MIKE CORCORAN, a director

RALPH RACKSTRAW, a writer

DICK LIVE-EYE, an agent

BRENDA BLOSSOM, a star

LOUHEDDA HOPSONS, a columnist

BOB BECKET, a press agent

MISS HEBE, Mr. Porter's secretary

ACTORS, ACTRESSES, WRITERS, OTHER WORKERS IN THE STUDIO

THE SCENE

Office of Pinafore, Pictures, Hollywood.

ACT ONE: Day.

ACT TWO: Evening.

HOLLYWOOD PINAFORE

Or The Lad Who Loved A Salary

ACT ONE

The scene is the office of Pinafore Pictures, Hollywood. A gorgeous room — the walls are done in grey satin and red marble. Up center three archways and a domed ceiling. A center stairway leads to two balconies right and left. This, of course, is the "Poop Deck" of Pinafore.

On each balcony there is a door. Two curbed desks are formed by the curving rails of the stairway leading right and left. On each desk are three telephones of varying colors, and back of each desk is a beautiful blonde. There is a uniformed Doorman at the center door. Six Pageboys are posed down front — Actors and Actresses in various costumes are arranged on steps.

The opening scene is played with music under it, and to the incessant movement, up and down stairs, in and out of doors, of Pages and various Actors, Actresses and Executives.

Both Secretaries are speaking alternately on the telephones as the curtain rises.

ENSEMBLE

SECRETARIES.
> Pinafore Pictures!
> Pinafore Pictures!
> Pinafore Pictures!
> Pinafore Pictures!
> Mr. Joseph Porter?
> Mr. Joseph Porter?

Mr. Porter's in the projector's room!

Mr. Porter's in the projector's room!

Mr. Porter's in the projector's room!

An Egyptian mummy on Stage 12. Must be female!

An Egyptian mummy on Stage 12. Must be female!

Pinafore Pictures!

Pinafore Pictures!

Try Selznick!

Try Metro!

Try Goldwyn!

Try Zanuck!

Mr. Porter is in his private bungalow!

Mr. Porter is in his private bungalow!

Try Warners!

Try Paramount!

Try Monogram!

Try Republic!

Mr. Porter is in the barber shop!

Mr. Porter is in the barber shop!

Pinafore Pictures!

Pinafore Pictures!

Pinafore Pictures!

Pinafore Pictures!

Pinafore Pictures!

Pinafore Pictures!!!!

CHORUS.
> WE ARE SIMPLE MOVIE FOLK
> > OF THE WOOD THAT'S KNOWN AS HOLLY;
> AND WE LIGHTLY BEAR THE YOKE
> > OF A LIFE OF LOVELY FOLLY.
> WE GO TO WORK AT DAWN
> > AND WE CARRY ON
> TILL THE COOL OF THE EVENING COMES;
> > WE'RE IN THE ERMINE AND JADE,

FOR WE ALL GET PAID
TERRIFICALLY FANCY SUMS
OH, JOY! OH, JOY!

WE GO TO WORK AT DAWN
OH JOY, OH JOY, AND WE CARRY ON
CARRY ON, TILL THE COOL OF THE EVENING COMES.

WE ARE SIMPLE MOVIE FOLK
OF THE WOOD THAT'S KNOWN AS HOLLY;
AND WE LIGHTLY BEAR THE YOKE
OF A LIFE OF LOVELY FOLLY.
WE WORK FROM EARLY DAWN,
TILL THE COOL OF THE EVENING COMES
FOR WE GET PAID TERRIFICALLY FANCY SUMS.

DOORMAN.
MISS GLORIA MUNDI — $1500 A WEEK.

(Miss Gloria enters U.C. — dressed in black sequins.)

GLORIA.
I AM SIMPLE MOVIE FOLK
OF THE WOOD THAT'S KNOWN AS HOLLY

CHORUS.
AND WE LIGHTLY BEAR THE YOKE
OF A LIFE OF LOVELY FOLLY.

GLORIA.
ON A WAGE SO LOW
I AM PLUNGED IN WOE
A MOST UNHAPPY MISS
I MUST GO BARE
OR ELSE JUST WEAR
A MISERABLE RAG LIKE THIS.

CHORUS.

    SHE MUST GO BARE, OR ELSE JUST WEAR
        A MISERABLE RAG LIKE THIS.

DOORMAN.

    MISS BEVERLY WILSHIRE — $5,000 PER WEEK.

(Miss Beverly enters U.C. — Tall blonde dressed in slacks and white blouse, dragging a mink coat behind her.)

BEVERLY.

    I AM SIMPLE MOVIE FOLK
    OF THE WOOD THAT'S KNOWN AS HOLLY

CHORUS.

    AND SHE LIGHTLY BEARS THE YOKE
    OF A LIFE OF LOVELY FOLLY.

BEVERLY.

    MINE'S A NAME YOU OFTEN SEE
    UP IN LIGHTS ON A MARQUEE
    FOR A GLITTERING STAR AM I
    IF YOU CARE TO TAKE A GUESS
    AT THE CAUSE OF MY SUCCESS
    THERE'RE TWO LITTLE REASONS WHY.

CHORUS.

    OH YES, OH YES.
    CAUSE OF HER SUCCESS,
    OH YES, OH YES.
    THERE'S TWO LITTLE REASONS WHY.

DOORMAN.

    MISS PEGGY — $8,000 PER WEEK.

(Miss Peggy enters U.C. — dressed like a girl of six.)

PEGGY.

    I AM SIMPLE MOVIE FOLK
    OF THE WOOD THAT'S KNOWN AS HOLLY

CHORUS.

    AND SHE LIGHTLY BEARS THE YOKE

    OF A LIFE OF LOVELY FOLLY.

PEGGY.

    FOR A LITTLE GIRL OF SIX

    I HAVE QUITE A BAG OF TRICKS

    I'M SWEET IN A FAUNTLEROY SUIT;

    I AM VERY GOOD FOR BIZ,

    AND THE REASON IS:

        I'M TERRIBLY GODDAMN CUTE!

CHORUS.

    VERY GOOD, VERY GOOD FOR BIZ — GOOD FOR BIZ —

    FOR SHE IS SO GODDAMN CUTE.

DOORMAN.

    SILVER TASSEL — $10,000 PER WEEK.

(Page Boy enters U.C. — leading Collie on jewelled leash.)

CHORUS.

    WE ARE SIMPLE MOVIE FOLK

        OF THE WOOD THAT'S KNOWN AS HOLLY;

    AND WE LIGHTLY BEAR THE YOKE

        OF A LIFE OF LOVELY FOLLY.

    BUT BEFORE WE GO AWAY

    WE HAVE THIS TO SAY,

        OF AN AUTHOR WORLD-RENOWNED:

    MR. GILBERT IF HE KNEW

    WHAT WE'RE GOING TO DO

        WOULD BE WHIRLING ROUND AND ROUND.

    OH BOY, OH BOY, BEFORE WE GO AWAY

    OH JOY, OH JOY, WE HAVE THIS TO SAY

    HE'D BURROW IN THE COLD, COLD GROUND.

    WE ARE SIMPLE MOVIE FOLK

        OF THE WOOD THAT'S KNOWN AS HOLLY;

AND WE LIGHTLY BEAR THE YOKE
    OF A LIFE OF LOVELY FOLLY.
WE WORK FROM EARLY DAWN
TILL THE COOL OF EVENING COMES
FOR WE GET PAID TERRIFICALLY FANCY SUMS.

(Three stars and eight men exit on both sides. Telephone rings.)

1ST SECRETARY.   Pinafore Pictures.

2ND SECRETARY.   Pinafore Pictures.

1ST SECRETARY.   Mr. Porter's looking at the rushes.

2ND SECRETARY.   Mr. Porter's looking at the rushes.

DOORMAN.   Hollywood's greatest columnist! Miss Louhedda Hopsons!

(Louhedda enters U.C. A buxom woman, draped in jewels and carrying a basket in which are folded newspapers and carrying a pencil and small notebook.)

SECRETARIES.   *(Alternately.)* Lassie — Louhedda!

LOUHEDDA.   *(Recitative.)*
    Hail, Pinafore men! To Louhedda hearken!
    Brief is my stay — I found no place to park in.
    Pray hold naught back! I've come to gather news.
    You'd be surprised the drivel I can use!

(Actors and Actresses flock in, chattering with excitement.)

ALL BUT LOUHEDDA.   Louhedda! Lassie!

LOUHEDDA.   My merry friends!

ALL BUT LOUHEDDA.   Have you news for us? Aye, Louhedda, what have you to tell us?

LOUHEDDA.   Ah, for that you must buy my papers! *(Hands each group a newspaper.)*

I'VE WONDERFUL STORIES OF HOLLYWOOD'S GLORIES,
    TO MELLOW YOUR LITTLE INSIDES;
I'VE NEWS OF DIVORCES, AND LOUIS MAYER'S HORSES,
    AND JUST WHO ARE GOING TO BE BRIDES.
I'M CZAR AND CZARINA OF THIS ENTIRE SCENA,
    AND HERE IS MY POLICY TRUE:
IF YOU'LL BUTTER *ME* UP, NOT GIVE ME THE KNEE UP,
    THEN I'LL GLADLY BUTTER UP *YOU.*

I'M CALLED LITTLE BUTTER-UP, DEAR LITTLE BUTTER-UP;
    GOOD REASON WHY IT SHOULD BE;
THE PAGES I CLUTTER UP, MUSH THAT I UTTER UP —
    SWEET LITTLE BUTTER-UP, ME!

It should of course be "I," but my English is not of the best.

ALL BUT LOUHEDDA.
    SHE'S CALLED LITTLE BUTTER-UP, DEAR LITTLE BUTTER-UP
    GOOD REASON WHY IT SHOULD BE!
    THE PAGES SHE'LL CLUTTER UP, MUSH THAT SHE'LL UTTER UP —
    SWEET LITTLE BUTTER-UP, SHE!

LOUHEDDA.
    HER!

ALL BUT LOUHEDDA.
    SHE!

LOUHEDDA.
    AH, WELL! HAVE IT THEN YOUR WAY!

ALL BUT LOUHEDDA.
    BUT YOU HAVE FAILED TO TELL US NEWS, DEAR LOUHEDDA!

MISS GEORGE.
    YOU HAVE IMPARTED NO NEWS!

LOUHEDDA.
>LAST NIGHT, SEEKING TOPICS, I WENT TO THE TROPICS
>>AND GOT A MOST WONDERFUL BREAK.
>I KNOW WHO WAS SITTIN' WITH BARBARA BRITTON,
>>AND ALSO VERONICA LAKE.
>POOR RITA'S DIVORCIN' THAT AWFUL MAN ORSON
>>(I'M MAKING THAT UP TO PLEASE HEARST);
>AND ALICE FAYE MAY BE EXPECTING A BABY
>>A YEAR FROM NEXT OCTOBER FIRST!
>>"THAT'S EXCLUSIVE"

ALL BUT LOUHEDDA.
>SHE'S CALLED LITTLE BUTTER-UP, DEAR LITTLE BUTTER-UP
>>GOOD REASON WHY IT SHOULD BE;
>THE PAGES SHE'LL CLUTTER UP, MUSH THAT SHE'LL UTTER UP,
>>SWEET LITTLE BUTTER-UP, SHE!

(Louhedda chimes in <u>SHE</u>.)

LOUHEDDA.
>MY MERE DISAPPROVAL CAN MEAN YOUR REMOVAL;
>>TAKE CARE NOT TO MERIT MY SCORN;
>SO YOU WHO HAVE KNOWN ME WILL DO WELL TO PHONE ME
>>BEFORE YOU GET MARRIED OR BORN.

ALL BUT LOUHEDDA.
>SHE'S CALLED LITTLE BUTTER-UP, DEAR LITTLE BUTTER-UP
>>GOOD REASON WHY IT SHOULD BE.

LOUHEDDA.
>WORDS SHE WILL SPLUTTER UP
>>NO ONE CAN SHUT HER UP
>SWEET LITTLE BUTTER-UP, ME!

(Secretaries sit down. All exit except Louhedda — she's D.C. slightly L.)

DOORMAN.

   Mr. Bob Becket! Public Relations Council.

(Bob Becket enters U.C. Carries newspapers, clippings, magazines. To Secretaries.)

BOB.   Good morning, good morning. Ah, Louhedda *(Goes D.R. of Louhedda.)* I have but learned of your presence!

LOUHEDDA.   Good Bob, pray have you news for me? *(She whips out pad and pencil.)*

BOB.   I have indeed. *(Lowers his voice.)* The studio is bent upon a film of unusual splendor. Mr. Porter, for untold thousands, has purchased the motion picture rights to "The Raven" by Poe.

LOUHEDDA.   *(Doubtfully.)* By who? *(She writes.)*

BOB.   Edgar Allen Poe.

LOUHEDDA.   Oh the Italian — but stay! It matters not who *writes* a picture. *(She erases her notes.)* Who the *star* who will appear in it?

BOB.   Ah! *(Very secretly.)* Brenda Blossom! *(Stands back to catch effect — a quick look off.)*

LOUHEDDA.   Brenda Blossom!

BOB.   *(Crosses L.)* Say too that Poe's "The Raven" will be photographed in glorious Technicolor, from a screenplay by Ralph Rackstraw.

LOUHEDDA.   *(Recoiling.)* Ralph Rackstraw.... Hark ye, good Bob! Hast ever thought that beneath a gay and frivolous exterior there may lurk a canker worm which is slowly but surely eating its way into my very heart? What then would you say?

BOB.   *(Looking at her ample bosom.)* I'd say he had quite a way to go.

DOORMAN.   Mr. Richard Live-eye. Agent! Ten percent of everybody's salary.

DICK. *(To the Doorman — enters U.C. The newcomer is dressed to kill, but with a patch over one eye, carrying his hat and gold cigarette case in pocket.)* Thank you.

BOB. Ah, Dick Live-eye!

LOUHEDDA. Dick darling!

DICK. Louhedda!

BOB. But what has happened?

DICK. I received it from a client. 'Tis but ten percent of what *he* got. *(To Secretary at R. desk.)* My pretty one, wilt call New York for me upon the telephone?

2ND SECRETARY. Aye, sir. With whom would you speak?

DICK. *(Fast.)* The City of New York. *(Crosses C. again.)*

LOUHEDDA. Hast news for me, Dick?

DICK. That I have indeed. But yesternight I was engaged in a gin rummy with David Selznick —

LOUHEDDA. *(Her notebook ready.)* David Selznick! What said he?

DICK. He said "If you schneider me again I'll have you barred from the studio."

2ND SECRETARY. Pray hold the line. It is New York, Mr. Live-eye.

DICK. Hello! ... New York? ... What time is it? ... Thanks. *(Hangs up.)* Get me ORSON WELLES! *(To the other Secretary.)* Get me the race track, I want to talk to my horse. There must be somebody there. I'm so busy I don't know what to do next!

BOB. Didst know, Louhedda, that we are today shooting some underwater scenes?

LOUHEDDA. *(Crosses R.)* Under water? I shall drop in. *(Exits D.R.)*

BOB. Well, Dick, what's the news?

DICK. I just put through the biggest deal of my life! I sold Warner Brothers the motion picture rights to the Bible!

BOB. Where did *you* get them?

DICK. What's the difference? I *sold* them! And I just sold Clark Gable to Metro!

BOB. But Metro already *has* Clark Gable.

DICK. They forgot all about it. I got him the best deal of his career — a million dollars a minute! And I get ten percent! That's what agents are for — to get ten percent! But what happens? They don't appreciate me! They bar me from the studios!

BOB. Are you not barred from this studio?

DICK. Aye, Lad. I'm barred from every studio. *(Three boys enter L. — three enter R. Four Pages enter U.C. Each carries cigarette and money.)* From every restaurant! From every home! From the A&P. And know why? Because I am an agent! I am hated by all! Do you not all hate me?

ALL. We do!

DICK. Because I get ten percent! But you don't know what I have to go through. You don't know what I have to go through to sell you. *(Bob exits D.L.)*

DICK and CHORUS

> WHEN AN AGENT'S NOT ENGAGED IN HIS EMPLOYMENT —
> > HIS EMPLOYMENT —
> OR PREPARING HIS FELONIOUS LITTLE PLANS —
> > LITTLE PLANS —
> HIS CAPACITY FOR INNOCENT ENJOYMENT —
> > INNOCENT ENJOYMENT —
> IS JUST AS GREAT AS ANY HONEST MAN'S —
> > HONEST MAN'S —
> HIS SYMPATHETIC HEART HE HAS TO SMOTHER —
> > HAS TO SMOOTHER —

WHEN DIRTY WORK IS ACHING TO BE DONE —
                    TO BE DONE —
TAKING ONE CONSIDERATION WITH ANOTHER —
                    WITH ANOTHER —
AN AGENT'S LIFE IS NOT A HAPPY ONE —
                    HAPPY ONE.

CHORUS.
    WHEN DIRTY WORK IS ACHING TO BE DONE, TO BE DONE,
    AN AGENT'S LOT IS NOT A HAPPY ONE.

(Dick passes hat and they all drop money in.)

DICK and CHORUS.
    HE MUST WORK FROM TWELVE TO ONE FOR ALL THAT'S IN IT —
                    ALL THAT'S IN IT —
    IF HE RINGS A BELL A TALL BRUNETTE RESPONDS —
                    'NETTE RESPONDS —
    IF HE ONLY LEAVES HIS OFFICE FOR A MINUTE —
                    FOR A MINUTE —
    HE IS CHASED BY SIXTY-SEVEN GORGEOUS BLONDES —
                    GORGEOUS BLONDES.
    ONE WILL KISS HIM FOR SOME FAVOR THAT HE DID HER —
                    THAT HE DID HER —
    AND ANOTHER THINKS IT MIGHT BE LOTS OF FUN —
                    LOTS OF FUN —
    IF YOU REALLY STOP AND CAREFULLY CONSIDER —
                    'LY CONSIDER —
    AN AGENT'S LOT IS NOT A HAPPY ONE —
                    HAPPY ONE.

    YES, ANOTHER THINKS IT MIGHT BE LOTS OF FUN,
        LOTS OF FUN —
    AN AGENT'S LOT IS NOT A HAPPY ONE.

(Dick passes his gold cigarette case and each Boy puts a cigarette in.)

HE MUST LUNCH WITH EITHER GRABLE OR WITH HEDY —

OR WITH HEDY —

HE MUST DINE WITH MARLENE DIETRICH OR BACALL —

OR BACALL —

HE IS MADE TO GO WITH BETTY HUTTON STEADY —

HUTTON STEADY —

HE JUST NEVER SEES A HOMELY GIRL AT ALL —

GIRL AT ALL.

HE MUST MOTOR OUT TO ALL THE PRIVATE BEACHES —

PRIVATE BEACHES —

HE IS FORCED TO LIE A BASKING IN THE SUN —

IN THE SUN —

HE WOULD LIKE THAT IF YOU WERE IN HIS BREECHES —

IN HIS BREECHES —

AN AGENT'S LOT IS NOT A HAPPY ONE — HAPPY ONE.

CHORUS.

HE IS FORCED TO LIE A BASKING IN THE SUN, IN THE SUN —

AN AGENT'S LOT IS NOT A HAPPY ONE.

(All Boys exit. Bob reenters U.L. Louhedda enters U.C. Bob comes D.C.)

LOUHEDDA.   *(In front of L. desk.)* But tell me! Who's the youth upon yon spot? What is his name? Pray, tell who he might be!

BOB.   That is the smartest writer on the lot — Ralph Rackstraw!

LOUHEDDA.   Ralph! That name! Ah, woe is me. *(Louhedda exits U.R. — Bob exits D.L.)*

DOORMAN.   *(Announcing.)* Ralph Rackstraw! Writer! 75 dollars a week! *(Doorman exits disgustedly — Actors and Actresses enter both sides and on balcony. Ralph enters U.C. He wears convict stripes. Holding script. All turn their backs.)*

19

RALPH.   *(Coming D.C.)*

> WHEREVER I ROAM ONE AND ALL TURN AWAY
>> THEY DARE NOT FACE THOSE WHO GAIN SUCH
>>> TRIVIAL PAY
> THEY SING "HOW MUCH A DAY?"

CHORUS.

> THEY SING "HOW MUCH A DAY?"

RALPH.

> ALAS, WHERE IS MY SHARE OF ADMIRATION?
>> MINE IS A LIFE OF SITTING IN THE GALL'RY.
> O'ERLAID WITH GRIEVOUS PAIN MY SITUATION;
>> I LOVE — AND LOVE, ALAS, ABOVE MY SAL'RY.

GIRL.

> HE LOVES — AND LOVES A LASS ABOVE HIS SAL'RY.

PAMELA.

> YES, YES — THE LASS IS MUCH ABOVE HIS SAL'RY.

RALPH.

> A MAIDEN OFTEN SEEN
> UPON THE SILVER SCREEN,
>> BEWITCHING, FAIR, AND THRILLING;
> FOR WHOM PRODUCERS SIGH
> AND WITH EACH OTHER VIE
>> TO GIVE HER BIGGER BILLING.

ALL.

> TO GIVE HER BIGGER BILLING.

RALPH.

> A WRITER, LOWLY PAID,
> MAYN'T HOPE FOR SUCH A MAID;
>> I CURSE HER EV'RY DAMN BEAU.
> MY LIFE CAN NE'ER BE HERS;

I CANNOT BUY RICH FURS,
 NOR TAKE HER TO MOCAMBO.

ALL.
 NOR TAKE HER TO MOCAMBO.

RALPH.
 SINCE FIRST I FELL IN LOVE
 WITH ONE SO FAR ABOVE,
  I'M TWENTY-TWO POUNDS LIGHTER.
 OH, PITY, PITY ME!
 A MOVIE STAR IS SHE!
 AND I AM A LOWLY WRITER.

CHORUS and RALPH.
 OH, PITY, PITY ME!
 A MOVIE STAR IS SHE!
 AND I AM A LOWLY WRITER.
 AND HE, AND HE A LOWLY WRITER.

(Bob enters D.L. Chorus exits.)

BOB. Ah, my poor lad, my poor lad. *(Dick enters D.R.)*

DICK. Brave lad, I know you not. I know not *any* writers. But I would give you some advice — if you would wed Brenda Blossom, make of yourself *anything* but a writer — anything! 'Tis your only chance.

RALPH. But, I *am* a writer. What else can I be?

DICK. It matters not. The maidens of this town marry producers, executives, directors, actors, cameramen, makeup men, clothes designers, scene designers, insurance men, doctors and dogcatchers, but they do *not* marry writers.

RALPH. But *somebody* has to marry writers.

DICK. I see no reason.

RALPH. I understand.... *(Phone rings. Ralph exits D.R.)*

RIGHT SECRETARY. Hello — Just a minute. 'Tis Orson Welles.

DICK. Hello — Orson? How's Rita? Good. *(He hangs up.)* Tell me, Bob, where is Peggy working?

BOB. Miss Peggy? The child star? Stage eight. I'll show you.

DICK. I've got to see her. I have a message for her from Errol Flynn. *(Bob and Dick exit D.L.)*

DOORMAN. Mr. Michael Corcoran, director. 500,000 a year, under a capital gains setup! *(Corcoran enters U.C. Chorus enters.)*

CORCORAN. My boys and girls, good morning!

ALL but CORCORAN.
  SIR, GOOD MORNING!

CORCORAN.
  ARE YOU READY FOR A TAKE?

ALL but CORCORAN.
  WE ARE, AND RETAKES!

CORCORAN.
  WHY DO YOU LAUGH AT ALL MY JOKES, AND LISTEN TO
    MY DULL STO-RIES?

ALL but CORCORAN.
  YOU'RE THE DI-REC-TOR!

CORCORAN.
  I'M A BIG DIRECTOR AT PINAFORE.

ALL but CORCORAN.
  AND A GOOD DIRECTOR, TOO.

CORCORAN.
  AND I PUT IT AS A FACT
  THAT MOST OF YOU CAN ACT

22

AS WELL AS A KANGAROO.
WHEN IT SAYS "DIRECTED BY"
THEN MY ALL-OBSERVING EYE
HAS WATCHED EV'RY LIGHT AND PROP;
EV'RY PICTURE FROM MY HAND
BREAKS THE RECORD AT THE STRAND
AND I NEVER, NEVER MAKE A FLOP.

ALL but CORCORAN.
WHAT, NEVER?

CORCORAN.
NO, NEVER!

ALL but CORCORAN.
WHAT, NEVER?

CORCORAN.
WELL, HARDLY EVER!

ALL but CORCORAN.   (*Three Cheerleaders enter D.L. with sweaters and mega-phones initialed "P.P."*)
HE HARDLY EVERY MAKES A FLOP
    THEN GIVE THREE CHEERS AND ONE CHEER MORE
    FOR THE BEST DIRECTOR HERE AT PINAFORE!
THEN GIVE THREE CHEERS FOR A *WONDERFUL* DIRECTOR!

CORCORAN.
MY PICTURES ALWAYS TELL A SIMPLE TALE —

ALL but CORCORAN.
WE ARE HANGING ON YOUR EV'RY PHRASE.

CORCORAN.
EVERY EPISODE IS PLANNED
FOR A CHILD TO UNDERSTAND,
    AND I WORSHIP MR. WILL H. HAYES.

IF TWO PEOPLE ARE IN BED
  THEY MUST BOTH BE WED OR DEAD.
IT'S A PROPER WILL H. HAYS DECREE;
  I DEFER TO HIS UKASE
  ON THE LENGTH OF AN EMBRACE,
AND I NEVER USE A BIG, BIG D.

ALL BUT CORCORAN.
 WHAT, NEVER?

CORCORAN.
 NO, NEVER!

ALL BUT CORCORAN.
 WHAT, *NEVER?*

CORCORAN.
 ONLY IN *GONE WITH THE WIND.*

ALL BUT CORCORAN.
 HARDLY EVER USE A BIG, BIG D.
 THEN GIVE THREE CHEERS AND ONE CHEER MORE
 FOR A *CLEAN* DIRECTOR HERE AT PINAFORE!
 THEN GIVE THREE CHEERS FOR A *NICE CLEAN* DIRECTOR!

(All go out except Corcoran.)

CORCORAN. Stage eight ready.

LEFT SECRETARY. *(At L. desk.)* Yes, Mr. Corcoran.

CORCORAN. *(Pacing D.)* Remember, I need a lavender rhinoceros at 4 o'-clock.

LEFT SECRETARY. Yes, Mr. Corcoran.

CORCORAN. And I want to see a print of *Sex Marches On. (Enter Louhedda U.C.)*

LOUHEDDA. *(Recitative.)*

    Mike, what's the news? You seem depressed and low —

    A mood that ill becomes a great director,

    Perhaps you have not had your morning coffee,

    Or maybe you've been looking at the rushes.

CORCORAN.

    Yes, Little Butter-Up, I am despondent,

    My daughter Josephine, who for some damn

    Fool reason changed her name to Brenda Blossom,

    Is sought in lawful marriage by Joe Porter,

    But she won't even go with him to Chasen's

    Or Lucey's, Romanoff's or the Brown Derby.

LOUHEDDA.

    Ah, poor Joe Porter! Ah, but sadder still,

    The fact that I can't print it in my column!

    But, see, here comes your most attractive daughter!

    That's all today! See you tomorrow!

(Passionately.)

    AH!

(She goes U.R.)

CORCORAN. *(Looking after her.)*

    A plump and wheezing person.

(He goes D.R. Enter Brenda, D.L. — in white hooped-skirt costume.)

BRENDA

    HERE ON THE LOT I AM A STAR,

        WHAT HAVE I GOT THAT OTHERS LONG FOR?

    BEAUTIFUL HOUSE, AND HANDSOME CAR —

        EVERYTHING BUT THE LAD I'M STRONG FOR.

    HERE ON THE LOT I AM A STAR

        WHAT HAVE I GOT THAT OTHERS LONG FOR.

HEAVY THE SORROW THAT BOWS THE HEAD
    WHEN LOVE IS ALIVE AND HOPE IS DEAD.
WHEN LOVE IS ALIVE AND HOPE IS DEAD.
    DAILY I KISS THE LEADING MAN
HOLDING HIM CLOSE IN SOFT EMBRACES,
    THINKING OF RALPH AS HARD AS I CAN,
THINKING HOW SWEET HIS DARLING FACE IS.
    DAILY I KISS THE LEADING MAN,
HOLDING HIM CLOSE IN SOFT EMBRACES,
    HEAVY THE SORROW THAT BOWS THE HEAD
WHEN LOVE IS ALIVE AND HOPE IS DEAD.
    WHEN LOVE IS ALIVE AND HOPE IS DEAD.

(Corcoran returns.)

CORCORAN.   Josephine, my child —

BRENDA. Nay, not Josephine, father. Brenda.

CORCORAN.   Brenda, then. My child, you are a prey to melancholy. Why? There are no heights to which you cannot ascent, if you give ear to the pleadings of Joe Porter. *(Goes R.)*

BRENDA. Ah, father, your words cut me to the quick. I can esteem — reverence — venerate Joe Porter, for he is a great and good man, but I cannot love him. My heart is already given.

CORCORAN.   It is then as I feared.... Given to whom? Not to some foppish actor?

BRENDA. No, father, the object of my love is no actor. Oh, pity me, for he is but a humble writer.

CORCORAN.   A *writer!* Oh, fie! What hath this lad written?

BRENDA.   But little, father. Only a celluloid in which Roy Rogers did appear.

CORCORAN.   Roy? Not Ginger?

BRENDA. Nay, not Ginger. But at this moment, he labors upon a work of great import. He is writing Poe's "The Raven" for *me*, father.

CORCORAN. Be not too certain. *(Crosses D.L.)* For if you do not wed with Joe Porter — *(He breaks off. Crosses back to her.)* — but tell me, how did you meet with this writer? Writers are held within a structure of their own — they are not permitted to stray from it.

BRENDA. I know, father. But my steps took me near to the building in which the writers labor, and suddenly a voice came to me, and I looked up. there was his face, pressed against the bars. He was crying, "Let me out of here! I'm just as sane as you are!" You know, father, I think he *is* just as sane as we are.

CORCORAN. But stop and think, my child. Why then did they put him *in* there? Surely there was reason.

BRENDA. I blush for the weakness that allows me to cherish such a passion. But I love him! I love him! I love him!

CORCORAN. Come, my child. In a matter of the heart I would not coerce my daughter — I attach but little value to rank *or* wealth. But a writer! The line must be drawn somewhere.

BRENDA. Fear not, father. I have a heart, and therefore I love, but I am a star, and I have won the Academy Award, and therefore I am proud. What was it Gilbert said? Though I carry my love with me to the West Hollywood Mortuary, he shall never know.

CORCORAN. You are my daughter, after all.... But hear, Joe Porter's car approaches, accompanied by the admiring crowd of sisters, cousins and aunts to whom he has given jobs in the studio. Retire, my daughter, to your dressing room — it may help to bring you to a more reasonable frame of mind.

BRENDA. My own thoughtful father. *(Corcoran and Brenda exit D.L. Chorus and Relatives: Male Chorus enters.)*

CHORUS.
> JOE PORTER'S CAR IS SEEN
>> WITH HENCHMEN GREAT AND LESSER,

THE RULER OF THE SCREEN,
     WHO ALWAYS GETS A "YES, SIR."
WE'RE SIMPLE, SIMPLE MOVIE FOLK,
     OF THE WOOD THAT'S KNOWN AS HOLLY;
WE LIGHTLY, LIGHTLY BEAR THE YOKE
     OF A LIFE OF LOVELY FOLLY.
LIGHTLY, LIGHTLY, BEAR THE YOKE.
     WE HAVE ALWAYS BOWED THE KNEE,
AND NAUGHT BUT PRAISE WE'VE UTTERED;
     YOU WILL READILY AGREE
WE KNOW WHICH SIDE WE'RE BUTTERED.

RELATIVES.   *(Dancers in yellow dresses. Girls in long and short slacks enter U.C.)*
GAILY TRIPPING,
LIGHTLY SKIPPING —
     RELATIVES ARE ALWAYS GYPPING
GAILY TRIPPING — LIGHTLY SKIPPING
     RELATIVES ARE ALWAYS GYPPING.

ACTORS.
     THIS AND THAT ONE THEY ARE CLIPPING;
     RARELY DO THEY DO THE TIPPING.

RELATIVES.
     ALWAYS BRIGHTLY
     CALLING NIGHTLY
          TALKING STEADILY AND TRITELY.

ACTORS.
     STATING ALL THINGS IMPOLITELY —
     WHY ARE MOST OF THEM UNSIGHTLY?
     MOST OF THEM UNSIGHTLY.
     ALWAYS BRIGHTLY CALLING
     NIGHTLY TALKING, STEADILY AND TRITELY
     GAILY TRIPPING, LIGHTLY SKIPPING
     RELATIVES ARE ALWAYS GYPPING.

RELATIVES.	CHORUS.
GAILY TRIPPING, LIGHTLY SKIPPING	WE HAVE ALWAYS BOWED THE KNEE
RELATIVES THEY ALWAYS GYP	AND NAUGHT BUT PRAISE
BRIGHTLY CALLING, NIGHTLY TALKING	WE'VE UTTERED
STEADILY AND TRITELY, OH SO TRITELY,	YOU WILL READILY AGREE
GAILY TRIPPING, LIGHTLY SKIPPING	WE KNOW WHICH SIDE WE'RE BUTTERED.
ALWAYS CALLING, TALKING	
STEADILY AND TRITELY.	

(Doorman U.C.)

DOORMAN.   Now give three cheers — I'll lead the way! Hurrah! Hurrah! Hurrah.

ACTORS and ACTRESSES.   Hurrah, Hurrah! Hurrah! *(Long, elaborate fanfare — all get down on their knees.)*

DOORMAN.   Mr. Joseph W. Porter, head of the studio! *Two million* dollars a year! Plus bonuses. *(Porter enters U.C. in high hat and tails — Miss Hebe dressed like him with large portfolio follows.)*

PORTER.   *(To Hebe.)* Am I in the right studio?

HEBE.   Yes, Mr. Porter.

PORTER.   *(Looks at the employees who are still on their knees.)* Arise, slaves! *(Takes a brief turn of inspection around the room.)* Miss Hebe.

HEBE.   Yes, Mr. Porter.

PORTER.   *(They both walk D.C.R.)* I'd like to get the afternoon light in this room. Will you see if you can arrange to have the sun set in the East after this?

HEBE.   I'll speak to someone. *(Song ... Porter, Hebe and Chorus.)*

PORTER.

    I AM THE MONARCH OF THE JOINT;

    ALL THAT I HAVE TO DO IS POINT.

        I PAY THE PIPER AND I CALL THE DANCE —

HEBE.

    AND WE ARE HIS SISTERS AND HIS COUSINS AND HIS AUNTS.

PORTER, HEBE, and CHORUS.

    AND WE ARE HIS SISTERS AND HIS COUSINS AND HIS AUNTS.

        HIS SISTERS AND HIS COUSINS AND HIS AUNTS.

PORTER.

    FOR WHEN A PICTURE'S FINE,

    THE CREDIT'S ALWAYS MINE,

        I GIVE MYSELF A BIG ADVANCE —

HEBE.

    AND SO DO HIS SISTERS AND HIS COUSINS AND HIS AUNTS.

PORTER, HEBE, and CHORUS.

    YES, SO DO HIS SISTERS AND HIS COUSINS AND HIS AUNTS.

        HIS SISTERS AND HIS COUSINS AND HIS AUNTS.

PORTER.

    BUT WHEN THE PREVIEW'S DREAR,

    I GENERALLY DISAPPEAR,

    AND SEEK THE SECLUSION THAT THE BATHROOM GRANTS —

HEBE.

    AND SO DO HIS SISTERS AND HIS COUSINS AND HIS AUNTS.

PORTER, HEBE, and CHORUS.

    YES, SO DO HIS SISTERS AND HIS COUSINS AND HIS AUNTS.

        AND SO HIS SISTERS AND HIS COUSINS AND HIS AUNTS.

           HIS SISTERS AND HIS COUSINS

           WHOM HE RECKONS UP BY DOZENS,

             AND HIS AUNTS.

PORTER. Hold. (*He motions forward the Secretary at L. desk. She comes D.C. to him.*) I've made another discovery. This girl can be a star.... Isn't it wonderful the way I keep on making discoveries?

HEBE. Yes, Mr. Porter.

PORTER. How many stars did I discover yesterday?

HEBE. Six, Mr. Porter.

PORTER. All girls.

HEBE. Yes sir.

PORTER. That's funny, isn't it?

HEBE. Yes, Mr. Porter.

PORTER. (*To Secretary at L. desk.*) What is your name?

HEBE. Pray.

PORTER. What's that?

HEBE. (*A heavy whisper.*) Pray....

PORTER. Oh, yes.... What is your name, pray?

LEFT SECRETARY. Bernice Greaseheimer.

PORTER. Bernice Greaseheimer ... that wouldn't look right on the marquee. Henceforth it will be ... (*He thinks.*) ... Sylvia Sin. You're going to be a star. Put on a bathing suit and have some stills taken.

LEFT SECRETARY. Yes, Mr. Porter.

PORTER. Then take off the bathing suit.

LEFT SECRETARY. Yes, Mr. Porter.

PORTER. And oh, yes ... pray.

LEFT SECRETARY. Yes, Mr. Porter.

PORTER. (*To Hebe.*) Get another girl to take her place.

31

HEBE. Yes, Mr. Porter. *(Snaps her fingers. A second beautiful blonde comes D.L. as Miss Greaseheimer leaves.)*

PORTER. Wait a minute. I'll make a star of her too. Get another girl. *(A third girl comes in.)*

HEBE. This is going to run into money.

PORTER. I'll wait a couple of weeks. Miss Hebe....

HEBE. Yes, Mr. Porter.

PORTER. Invite everyone to a party this evening, on stage one.

HEBE. Yes, Mr. Porter.

PORTER. We're going to barbecue an agent. There's too much competition here. All of you men get back to work.

ACTORS. Yes, Mr. Porter. *(All exit including Doorman.)*

PORTER. That's better. Wouldst you know how I got this way?
    WHEN I WAS A LAD I TRIED MY HAND
    AT EV'RY BUS-I-NESS IN THE LAND.
    MY LIST WAS MOST DIVERSIFIED —
    I SOLD UMBRELLAS AND INSECTICIDE.

CHORUS.
    HE SOLD UMBRELLAS AND INSECTICIDE.

PORTER.
    BUT I COULD NOT MAKE *ANYTHING* GO.
    SO NOW I AM THE RULER OF THE STUDIO.

CHORUS.
    BUT HE COULD NOT MAKE ANYTHING GO.
    SO NOW HE IS THE RULER OF THE STUDIO.

PORTER.
    I DROVE A TRUCK AND I WORKED IN A BANK,
    AND AT BOTH THOSE JOBS I *REALLY* STANK;
    I ALSO MADE ASBESTOS PIES,
    AND I MANUFACTURED ARTIFICIAL BUTTERFLIES.

CHORUS.

HE MANUFACTURED ARTIFICIAL BUTTERFLIES.

PORTER.

BUT IN ALL THAT TIME I NEVER SAID "NO,"
SO NOW I AM THE RULER OF THE STUDIO.

CHORUS.

BUT IN ALL THAT TIME HE NEVER SAID "NO,"
SO NOW HE IS THE RULER OF THE STUDIO.

PORTER.

AT GETTING TO JOBS I WAS OFTEN LATE,
BECAUSE OF WATCHING OTHER PEOPLE EXCAVATE
BUT I PROMPTLY ANSWERED EV'RY DINNER BELL,
AND I PLAYED A NIFTY HAND AT AUCTION PINCO*HELL*.

CHORUS.

AND HE PLAYED A NIFTY HAND AT AUCTION PINCOHELL.

PORTER.

WHICH MAKES IT HIGHLY APROPOS
THAT NOW I AM THE RULER OF THE STUDIO.

CHORUS.

WHICH MAKES IT HIGHLY APROPOS
THAT NOW HE IS THE RULER OF THE STUDIO.

PORTER.

I CLEANED THE WINDOWS AND I SCRUBBED THE FLOOR
OF A PLACE THAT I DON'T MENTION ANY MORE.
I WENT UPON THE STAGE AND DROPPED THE SPEAR,
AND I SAT UPON A BENCH IN CENTRAL PARK ONE YEAR.

CHORUS.

AND HE SAT UPON A BENCH IN CENTRAL PARK ONE YEAR.

PORTER.

BUT YOU OUGHTA SEE MY BUNGALOW
SINCE I BECAME THE RULER OF THE STUDIO.

CHORUS.

BUT YOU OUGHTA SEE HIS BUNGALOW

SINCE HE BECAME THE RULER OF THE STUDIO.

PORTER.

I GOT A JOB AS A SANDWICH MAN

BUT I FOUND THE WORK ENTIRELY TOO PEDESTRIAN;

I READ THE PICTURE MAGAZINES

AND I MADE A LOT OF MONEY PLAYING SLOT MACHINES.

CHORUS.

HE MADE A LOT OF MONEY PLAYING SLOT MACHINES.

PORTER.

I FLUNKED AS A BRAKEMAN ON THE B. AND O.

SO NOW I AM THE RULER OF THE STUDIO.

CHORUS.

HE FLUNKED AS A BRAKEMAN ON THE B. AND O.

SO NOW HE IS THE RULER OF THE STUDIO.

PORTER.

SO ALL SCHLEMIELS, WHOEVER YOU MAY BE,

IF YOU WANT TO RISE TO THE TOP OF THE TREE,

IF YOU WOULDN'T BE REGARDED AS A DARNED OLD FOOL,

BE CAREFUL TO BE GUIDED BY THIS GOLDEN RULE:

CHORUS.

BE CAREFUL TO BE GUIDED BY THIS GOLDEN RULE:

PORTER.

JUST TURN YOUR BACK 'NEATH THE MISTLETOE,

AND YOU ALL MAY BE RULERS OF THE STUDIO.

CHORUS.

JUST TURN YOUR BACK 'NEATH THE MISTLETOE,

AND YOU ALL MAY BE RULERS OF THE STUDIO.

(Exit Chorus. Corcoran enters U.C. and goes C. — Secretaries sit down.)

PORTER.

Oh, Mike!

CORCORAN.   Yes, Mr. Porter.

PORTER.   By chance this morning my eye fell upon the *Hollywood Reporter.* *(Hebe hands him a copy.)* It contains a most glowing editorial having to do with my genius. *(To Hebe.)* Be sure to read it. Remind me to take an eight-page ad.

HEBE.   Yes, Mr. Porter.

PORTER.   In color.

HEBE.   Yes, Mr. Porter.

PORTER.   With my picture in it.

HEBE.   Yes, Mr. Porter.

PORTER.   But 'tis not that of which I would speak. *(He tries this over.)* I speak would. *(Goes back to first way.)* Would speak.... It also refers to a certain group connected with the studio who are known as — what is the word again? *(He refreshes his memory from the paper.)* — "writers." Have we then such people?

CORCORAN.   Yes, sir.

PORTER.   Where are they? I fain would see one — fain.

CORCORAN.   *(Crosses D.R.)* Certainly, sir. *(He calls off R.)* Good ladies, pray this way. *(Hebe crosses behind them to L. of Porter. Eight writers shuffle in D.R., all in convict clothes and chained together at the feet. A uniformed Guard with a gun stands over them. Ralph Rackstraw leads them on.)*

GUARD.   *(As they march on.)* Hup! Pin-a-Fore. Hup! Pin-a-Fore. Hup! Pin-a-Fore. Halt!

PORTER.   Oh, so these are writers.

CORCORAN.   Yes, sir ... stand up straight. *(They make an attempt to do so.)*

PORTER.   Tell me, do you all have good sharp pencils — for writing?

RALPH and WRITERS.   Yes, sir. Yes, sir.

PORTER.   That's good. Are you writing good words?

RALPH and WRITERS.   We try to, sir. Yes, sir.

PORTER.   We want you to write good words, you know.

RALPH.   Yes, sir.

PORTER.   Are you all comfortable in that building?

RALPH.   Yes, sir. But if I might make a suggestion, sir?

PORTER.   Ho! A suggestion! From a writer Ho! This is going to be good. What is it?

RALPH.   *(Steps forward a step.)* If — if we could have a little more straw, sir.

PORTER.   Straw? To sleep on?

RALPH.   No, sir. To stuff the characters with, sir. One cannot make scripts without straw.

PORTER.   *(To Hebe.)* He kind of got me there. Do you get enough to eat?

RALPH.   Yes, sir. Plenty.

PORTER.   *(To Hebe.)* Try cutting it down a little. *(To Corcoran.)* And now, Mike, a word with you in my private office on a tender and sentimental subject. *Very* tender.

CORCORAN.   *(Reluctantly.)* I really should be shooting a scene, sir!

PORTER.   You can do that later. I want you *now*.

CORCORAN.   Yes, sir.

PORTER.   That's better. *(Arm-in-arm with Corcoran he heads D.R.)*
     FOR IN THIS STU-D-IO
     THE THINGS THAT I SAY *GO*.
          IN THIS SET-UP I WEAR THE PANTS —

HEBE.
     AND SO DO HIS SISTERS AND HIS COUSINS AND HIS AUNTS —

(They exit D.R. Porter and Hebe off — Corcoran going along — Bob enters D.L.)

RALPH.   *(Looking after Porter.)* The old poop!

36

WRITERS. *(In a line — facing Bob who is D.C.)* Well spoke! Well spoke!

BOB. Not so loud! Not so loud!

RALPH. *(Rallying the others around him.)* Mates, what say we dig a tunnel and escape?

WRITERS. Aye! Aye!

BOB. Careful! Careful!

RALPH. If once we get out of Hollywood we would be free men. It is the law.

WRITERS. Aye! Come!

BOB. Nay, nay! You cannot escape! Have they not options upon all of you?

WRITERS. *(Sadly.)* Aye!

RALPH. Aye.... Another Lincoln must arise to free us. *(Takes courage.)* But in one matter he cannot stop me. I'll speak to Brenda Blossom and tell her, like an honest man, of the love I have for her.

WRITERS. *(Advancing a step D.)* Aye, aye!

RALPH. Is not my love as good as another's? Is not my heart as true as another's? Have I not hands and eyes and ears and limbs like another, even though I am a writer?

WRITERS. Aye! Aye!

BOB. This is madness.... Come, let us sing the Studio Writers' Song. Perhaps it will bring this miserable creature to a proper state of mind. *(Song — Ralph, Bob, Guard and Chorus.)*

RALPH, BOB, GUARD and CHORUS.
> A WRITER FILLS THE LOWEST NICHE
> OF THE *ENTIRE* HUMAN SPAN;
> HE IS JUST ABOVE THE RAT AND SHOULD ALWAYS TIP HIS HAT
> WHEN HE MEETS THE GARBAGE MAN.

BOB and GUARD.

    HIS LIPS SHOULD TREMBLE

RALPH.

    AND HIS FACE SHOULD PALE

BOB and GUARD.

    HIS STEPS SHOULD FALTER

RALPH.

    AND HIS EYES SHOULD QUAIL

BOB and GUARD.

    HE SHOULD LIVE SOMEWHERE

RALPH.

    IN A 'DOBE HUT,

BOB, RALPH and GUARD.

    AND HE ALWAYS SHOULD BE READY FOR A SAL'RY CUT.

CHORUS.

    HIS LIPS SHOULD TREMBLE AND HIS FACE SHOULD PALE
    HIS STEPS SHOULD FALTER AND HIS EYES SHOULD QUAIL
    HE SHOULD LIVE SOMEWHERE IN A 'DOBE HUT,
    AND HE ALWAYS SHOULD BE READY FOR A SAL'RY CUT.

GUARD.

    PAGE ONE ... PAGE TWO

WRITERS.

    CUT THREE — INSERT.

GUARD.

    PAGE ONE ... PAGE TWO

WRITERS.

    CUT ... BOY MEETS GIRL!

RALPH.

    A WRITER DOES NOT OWN THE CHAINS
        THAT BIND HIM HEAD AND TOE;
    IF BEFORE HE FALLS ASLEEP HE SHOULD COUNT A LOT
      OF SHEEP,
        THEY BELONG TO THE STUDIO.

BOB and GUARD.

    HE SHOULD WORK EV'RY MORNING

RALPH.

    EV'RY NOON AND NIGHT

BOB and GUARD.

    AND ALL HE SHOULD DO

RALPH.

    IS WRITE AND WRITE

BOB and GUARD.

    TILL HE FALLS RIGHT OVER

RALPH.

    AND HIS EYES PROTRUDE

BOB, RALPH and GUARD.

    AND THIS SHOULD BE HIS CUSTOMARY ATTITUDE.

WRITERS.

(They kneel left knee.)

    HE SHOULD WORK EV'RY MORNING, EV'RY NOON AND NIGHT,
    AND ALL HE SHOULD DO IS WRITE AND WRITE
    TILL HE FALLS RIGHT OVER AND HIS EYES PROTRUDE,
    AND THIS SHOULD BE HIS CUSTOMARY ATTITUDE.
    HIS ATTITUDE, HIS ATTITUDE, HIS ATTITUDE.

GUARD.

    PAGE ONE ... PAGE TWO

WRITERS.

BACK TO THE MINES!

(Guard and Writers exits D.R.)

BOB.   *(Following them cracking imaginary whip.)* Hee — ho.... Hee — Ho. *(Doorman enters U.C. Porter enters D.R.)*

PORTER.   *(Crosses R. to Secretary.)* You don't mind if I stay out here a while?

LEFT SECRETARY.   Of course not, Mr. Porter.

PORTER.   Will it be all right with you?

RIGHT SECRETARY.   Yes, Mr. Porter.

PORTER.   My office is so big I can't see anybody. It gets lonesome. *(He wanders over to the Doorman.)* How much salary do you get?

DOORMAN.   Four-hundred dollars a week, sir.

PORTER.   Is that all?

DOORMAN.   Yes, sir.

PORTER.   And you have to stand here all day?

DOORMAN.   Yes, sir.

PORTER.   Would you like to be a motion picture star?

DOORMAN.   No, thank you, sir.

PORTER.   Why not?

DOORMAN.   You have to get up too early, sir. *(Porter nods, a Sweater Girl crosses from D.R. to out D.L.)*

PORTER.   Oh, Miss! Miss! Do you want to be — *(She is gone.)* Too late. She got away. *(Enter D.R. Bob, Assistant Director, Sylvia Sin.)*

BOB.   Here she is, Mr. Porter! All ready!

PORTER.   Who?

BOB.   Sylvia Sin!

PORTER.   Who's that?

BOB.   You made her a star — don't you remember? You *just* discovered her.

PORTER.   Oh, yes. So I did. I was smarter than I thought.

BOB.   Come on — everybody — Stage B, we're going to take some stills. *(To Porter.)* I'll put her face on every magazine cover in America.

PORTER.   Her what?

BOB.   I said, I'll put her face on every magazine cover in America.

PORTER.   Oh — well, that'll be nice too. *(Bob and group exit D.L. Doorman exits U.C. Dick Live-eye enters D.R.)*

DICK.   Hello there, Portie! Just the man I would see!

PORTER.   Who are you?

DICK.   Dick Live-eye — *you* remember. I'm an agent. We played hearts together at Sam Goldwyn's house.

PORTER.   Oh, yes. You gave me the queen of spades 12 times.

DICK.   I had to get rid of it.

PORTER.   That was the night I lost Gary Cooper. Sam Goldwyn won him.

DICK.   That's what I want to talk to you about. I fain would make amends.

PORTER.   Make what?

DICK.   Amends.

PORTER.   Oh!

DICK.   That means get you even.

PORTER. *(Gives him a look.)* Maybe we'd better leave it the way it is. *(Starts to go.)*

DICK. No, no. *(Bringing him back.)* I'm going to make a lot of money for you.

PORTER. Honest?

DICK. Well, *(Evasively.)* ... I want to be your agent.

PORTER. I don't like agents.

DICK. But I'm different. I'm working for *you.*

PORTER. But I get a lot of money now.

DICK. But you can get more if I'm your agent. I'll tell you what I'll do.... I'll give you ninety percent of everything you make.

PORTER. Ninety percent! Say, that's pretty good.

DICK. Then it's a deal?

PORTER. Sure! *(They shake hands.)*

DICK. Now to business? How about giving yourself a raise?

PORTER. All right. How much?

DICK. Oh, a million dollars. Remember, you get ninety percent.

PORTER. How much would that be?

DICK. Nine-hundred thousand dollars.

PORTER. Nine-hundred thousand dollars.

DICK. The tax on that is — let me see — *(He consults memorandum.)* — nine-hundred and *three* thousand dollars.

PORTER. Then I only lose three thousand dollars?

DICK. That's all.

PORTER. I'll do it!

DICK.   Great! *(They shake on it.)*

PORTER.   That's the best deal I made in a long time. You know, I didn't like you that other time. You scared me. That patch over your eye.

DICK.   Ho ho. That's the reason I wear it — to scare people.

PORTER.   That so?

DICK.   Sure! *(Takes it off.)* See? Nothing wrong at all.

PORTER.   Say!… Can I try it?

DICK.   Sure! *(Gives him patch.)*

PORTER.   *(Puts patch on.)* Now do I scare you?

DICK.   Sure you do!

PORTER.   I want to go around the studio and scare people.

DICK.   All right, Portie — you do that.

PORTER.   You know, if I had one on each eye I could scare people twice as much. *(He goes D.R.)*

DICK.   *(Calling after him.)* That's what you could! *(Dick looks surreptitiously around, slips on new eye cover.)*

LEFT SECRETARY.   Good sir, the business deal that you entered into with Mr. Porter … surely you too must pay a tax.

DICK.   I certainly must.

RIGHT SECRETARY.   Then will you not both lose money?

DICK.   That's what we will.

LEFT SECRETARY.   Pray why then do you do it?

DICK.   Why? Because it's Hollywood! Things aren't *supposed* to make sense in Hollywood! We're all crazy. Don't you know that! *(Song — Dick and Secretaries.)*

NEVER MIND THE WHY AND WHEREFORE!

THIS IS HOLLYWOOD AND THEREFORE

      WE'RE EXPECTED TO BE UTTERLY DEVOID OF THOUGHT

         OR CARE;

WE PUT KREML IN OUR BUTTER

      AND RUB SYRUP IN OUR HAIR!

WE ARE CRAZY, WE ARE CRAZY!

NOT A SINGLE THING WE KNOW!

AND WE PICK MANY A DAISY

      OUT A-STROLLING IN THE SNOW!

YET IN SPITE OF ALL THESE STRICTURES.

SECRETARIES.

     YES, IN SPITE OF ALL THESE STRICTURES,

(Girl crosses R. to L. — Makeup Man crosses R. to L. — as he passes her, he pulls her wig off and she screams and continues across in "bald" wig.)

DICK.

     WE TURN OUT THE DAMNEDEST PICTURES!

SECRETARIES.

     WE TURN OUT THE DAMNEDEST PICTURES.

(Girl in negligee crosses R. to L. — with script — rehearsing fainting scene.)

DICK.

     RING, PIANOS! WE ARE RAVY

         ALL ON MERRY MADNESS BENT!

WON'T YOU HAVE A PILE OF GRAVY?

         WON'T YOU EAT SOME NICE CEMENT?

(Sylvia Sin crosses with script on skates — L. to R.)

NEVER MIND THE WHY AND WHEREFORE!

THIS IS HOLLYWOOD AND THEREFORE

        IT'S A LEANING TOW'R OF BABEL

        THAT DELIGHTS IN CAVING IN!

EV'RY GIRL A BETTY GRABLE
EV'RY MAN AN ERROL FLYNN.

(Hebe crosses U.R. to L. — Tarzan crosses U.L. to R. — Hebe screams "Timber" as she passes him and chases him off U.R.)

WE ARE CRAZY, WE ARE CRAZY
    NOT A SINGLE THING WE KNOW!
AND WE PICK MANY A DAISY
    OUT A STROLLING IN THE SNOW!
GORGEOUS GIRLS AND MEN TO MATCH 'EM.

(Two Girls come out from either side — in shorts with books balanced on their heads.)

TWO GIRLS.
    GORGEOUS GIRLS AND MEN TO MATCH 'EM!

DICK.
    THEY RUN AFTER AND THEY *CATCH* 'EM!

TWO GIRLS.
    THEY RUN AFTER AND THEY *CATCH* 'EM!

(One Man crosses L. to R. with cake — another Man crosses from R. to L. talking to head on tray.)

DICK.
    RING, PIANOS, WE ARE DIPPY!
    WE PUT PEPPER IN OUR DRINKS!
    WON'T YOU JUMP THE MISSISSIPPI?
        WON'T YOU MANICURE THE SPHINX?

(Man walks from L. to R. in boat.)

NEVER MIND THE WHY AND WHEREFORE
THIS IS HOLLYWOOD AND THEREFORE
IT'S A GOLD-ENCRUSTED STEEPLE
    IN A DI'MOND COVERED TENT;
ANYONE RESEMBLING PEOPLE
    IS A NASTY ACCIDENT.

(Porter chases Sweater Girl R. to L.)

GIRLS.

    WE ARE CRAZY, WE ARE CRAZY!

      NOT A SINGLE THING WE KNOW!

    AND WE PICK MANY A DAISY

      OUT A STROLLING IN THE SNOW!

(Indian D.L. — Boy in angel suit D.R. Porter chases Girl back from U.L. to D.R.)

DICK.

    WE ARE MAD WITHIN THESE FENCES!

INDIAN and ANGEL.

    YES, WE'RE MAD WITHIN THESE FENCES!

(Hebe crosses U.R. to U.L. with Tarzan's leopard skin.)

DICK.

    HOPE WE DON'T REGAIN OUR SENSES!

INDIAN and ANGEL.

    HOPE WE DON'T REGAIN OUR SENSES!

(Beverly Wilshire crosses L. to R. in sequin dress carrying pail and mop.)

DICK.

    RING, PIANOS! WE ARE NUTTY!

      WE'VE ABANDONED EV'RY HOPE!

    WON'T YOU EAT A DISH OF PUTTY?

      WON'T YOU DRINK A GLASS OF SOAP?

(Man crosses R. to L. with goat. Secretaries and Dick exit. Ralph Rackstraw enters U.R. Then Brenda enters U.R.)

BRENDA.   *(As she sees him.)* Ralph Rackstraw!

RALPH.   Aye, lady — no other than poor Ralph Rackstraw.

BRENDA.   *(Aside.)* How my heart beats! *(Aloud.)* Have you yet finished your labors upon Poe's "The Raven."

RALPH.   Nay, not entirely. These matters take time.

BRENDA.   Tell me the part that I am to play.

RALPH.   'Twill be, of course, the title part, my lady. You will play "The Raven" — a private detective.

BRENDA.   I would fain hear more. *(Aside.)* My heart, my beating heart.

RALPH.   *(Suddenly.)* Brenda!

BRENDA.   *(Indignantly.)* Sir!

RALPH.   Brenda, I am a writer, and I love you.

BRENDA.   *(Aloud.)* Sir, this audacity! *(Aside.)* Oh my beating heart. *(Aloud.)* This unwarrantable presumption on the part of a common writer! You forget the gulf between us!

RALPH.   I forget nothing, haughty lady. I love you desperately, my life is in your hands. I have spoken and I await your word.

BRENDA.   You shall not wait long. Your proffered love I haughtily reject. Go, sir, and learn to cast your eyes upon some extra girl — they should be lowered before a star who has won the Academy Award!

RALPH and BRENDA.   *(Duet.)*
  REFRAIN, AUDACIOUS SCRIBE,
    YOUR SUIT FROM PRESSING.
 'TIS TIME YOU CEASED TO GIBE
    AND DID SOME YESSING.

  REFRAIN, AUDACIOUS SCRIBE,
    YOUR SUIT FROM PRESSING.
 'TIS TIME YOU CEASED TO GIBE
    AND DID SOME YESSING.

  REFRAIN, AUDACIOUS SCRIBE,
    REMEMBER WHAT YOU ARE.

RALPH.
  PROUD LADY, HAVE YOUR WAY,
    UNFEELING BEAUTY!

YOU SPEAK AND I OBEY
    IT IS MY DUTY!
FOR MINE THE LOWEST RUNG
    UPON THE LADDER;
THE WORDS YOU HAVE SUNG
    JUST MAKE ME SADDER.
PROUD LADY, HAVE YOUR WAY
YOU SPEAK, AND I OBEY

BRENDA.

    I'D SWALLOW MY DISTASTE IN UNION HOLY
    WERE HE MORE HIGHLY PLACED, AND I MORE LOWLY.

RALPH.

    MY HEART WITH ANGUISH TORN
        BOWS DOWN BEFORE HER.
    SHE LAUGHS MY LOVE TO SCORN
        YET I ADORE HER.

BRENDA.

    REFRAIN, AUDACIOUS SCRIBE, YOUR SUIT FROM PRESSING

RALPH.

    PROUD LADY, HAVE YOUR WAY, UNFEELING BEAUTY.

(Sung simultaneously.)

BRENDA.	RALPH.
I'D LAUGH MY RANK TO SCORN	PROUD LADY, HAVE YOUR WAY, UNFEELING BEAUTY
IN UNION HOLY, WERE HE MORE HIGHLY BORN	MY HEART WITH ANGUISH TORN BOWS DOWN BEFORE HER;
OR I MORE LOWLY.	SHE LAUGHS MY LOVE TO SCORN YET I ADORE HER.

RALPH.

    CAN I SURVIVE THIS OVERBEARING
    OR LIVE A LIFE OF MAD DESPAIRING,

MY PROFFERED LOVE DESPISED, REJECTED?
NO, NO, IT'S NOT TO BE EXPECTED.

(Calls off.)

GOOD FOLK, AHOY!
GIVE EAR, GIVE EAR!

(Enter Writers, Hebe, and Relatives.)

ALL but RALPH and BRENDA.
AYE, AYE, MY BOY!
WHAT CHEER, WHAT CHEER?
NOW TELL US, PRAY,
WITHOUT DELAY,
WHAT DOES SHE SAY?
WHAT CHEER, WHAT CHEER?

RALPH.   *(To Hebe.)*
MY OFFER BACK AT ME SHE HURLS
REJECTS MY HUMBLE GIFT, MY LADY.
REFERS ME TO THE EXTRA GIRLS
AND CUTS MY HOPES ADRIFT, MY LADY.

ALL but RALPH and BRENDA.
OH, CRUEL ONE! OH, CRUEL ONE!

(Dick suddenly appearing on the balcony L.)
SHE SPURNS YOUR SUIT? OHO! OHO!
I TOLD YOU SO! I TOLD YOU SO!

(Dick exits B.L.)

SHOULD HIS AFFECTION THUS BE KILLED?
A STAR IS SHE! OHO! OHO!
THIS GOES TO THE SCREEN WRITERS' GUILD
AND WILL THEY STAND FOR IT? OH, NO!

RALPH.   *(Hebe borrows Guard's gun, gives it to Ralph.)*
MY FRIENDS, MY LEAVE OF LIFE I'M TAKING,

FOR OH, MY HEART, MY HEART IS BREAKING.
WHEN I'M GONE, OH, PRITHEE TELL
THE MAID THAT, AS I DIED, I LOVED HER WELL!

BEHOLD, MY CELLMATES ALL
     WHO LOVE IN RANK ABOVE YOU —
FOR BRENDA DEAR I FALL —

(Puts gun to his head.)

BRENDA.   *(On balcony, L.)*
    STOP! STAY YOUR HAND! I LOVE YOU.

ALL but RALPH and BRENDA.
    AH, STAY YOUR HAND — SHE LOVES YOU!

RALPH.
    LOVES ME?

(Dick enters D.L.)

BRENDA.
    LOVES YOU!

ALL but RALPH and BRENDA.
    YES, YES ... AH, YES ... SHE LOVES YOU!

DICK.
    HE THINKS HE'S WON HIS BRENDA DEAR,
    BUT ME, I PERSONALLY FEAR
    A BIT OF THUNDER FROM ABOVE
    WILL END THEIR ILL-ASSORTED LOVE
        AND THWART THEIR DEAREST WISH.

    JOE PORTER ERE THE DAY IS DONE,
    WILL ALSO HAVE HIS LITTLE FUN.
    UNLESS ABSURDLY WRONG I AM
    THEY'LL ALL END UP AT MONOGRAM
        A PRETTY DISH OF FISH.

(Brenda and Ralph taking separate lines. Chorus repeats.)

BRENDA.

    THIS VERY NIGHT,

        MOST QUIET-LY

RALPH.

    WITH JUST THE RIGHT

        PUB-LIC-I-TY

BRENDA.

    A WEDDING BELL

        WILL SOUND ITS CHIMES —

RALPH.

    WE'LL ONLY TELL THE

        NEW YORK TIMES

BRENDA.

    WE SHALL BE ONE

        AT HALF PAST TEN

RALPH.

    AND THAT MEANS NONE

        CAN PART US THEN!

DICK.

    FORBEAR, ARE ALL OF YOU DEAF, DUMB AND BLIND?

    A WRITER MUST NOT PRODUCE HIS KIND!

    REMEMBER, SHE'S A STAR! A QUEEN OF SHEBA

    AND HE IS SOMEWHERE DOWN WITH THE AMEBA!

ALL but RALPH and BRENDA.

    BACK, AGENT, BACK!

        NOR MOCK US!

    BACK, AGENT, BACK!

        YOU SHOCK US!

    LET'S GIVE THREE CHEERS AND

    FOR THE WRITER'S BRIDE

WHO CASTS ALL COMMON SENSE ASIDE,
WHO CHOOSES HONEST LOVE TO SEEK
ON SEVENTY-FIVE BUCKS A WEEK!
TRA-LA-LA-LA *(ETC.)*

LET'S GIVE THREE CHEERS FOR THE WRITER'S BRIDE
WHO CASTS ALL COMMON SENSE ASIDE,
WHO CHOOSES HONEST LOVE TO SEEK
ON SEVENTY-FIVE BUCKS A WEEK!
TRA-LA-LA-LA *(ETC.)*

(Enter Porter D.R.)

PORTER.   Wait a minute! I don't know what this is all about, but nobody can get married on 75 dollars a week. I'm going to raise his salary.

ALL.   Hurrah!

DICK.   Good for you, Joe!

PORTER.   To *80* dollars a week!

ALL.   Hur ... aaah.

DICK.   80 bucks a week! And I get ten percent.

ALL.   Ssssssssss. *(First Act finale. Dick and Chorus — everyone.)*
A WRITER FILLS THE LOWEST NICHE
OF THE ENTIRE HUMAN SPAN,
HE IS JUST ABOVE THE RAT,
AND SHOULD ALWAYS TIP HIS HAT
WHEN HE MEETS THE GARBAGE MAN.
HE SHOULD WORK EVERY MORNING, NOON AND NIGHT
AND ALL HE SHOULD DO IS WRITE AND WRITE
TILL HE FALLS RIGHT OVER AND HIS EYES PROTRUDE.
AND THIS SHOULD BE HIS CUSTOMARY ATTITUDE.

BRENDA, HEBE, RALPH, and BOB.　CHORUS.

HIS WORDS SHOULD FLASH,　　　HIS ATTITUDE
OR HE GETS NO FOOD　　　　　 HIS ATTITUDE

HIS WORDS SHOULD FLASH　　　 HIS CUSTOMARY ATTITUDE
HIS WORDS SHOULD FLASH　　　 HIS ATTITUDE

OR HE GETS NO FOOD　　　　　 HIS ATTITUDE
HIS WORDS SHOULD FLASH

SHOULD FLASH　　　　　　　　 HIS WORDS, HIS WORDS
YES HIS WORDS SHOULD　　　　 YES, HIS WORDS, SHOULD
　　FLASH.　　　　　　　　　　　 FLASH.

(Two Page Boys bring in cashiers' desk D.R.)

ALL.

HE SHOULD WORK EVERY MORNING, EVERY NOON AND NIGHT.

BRENDA, HEBE, RALPH, and BOB.　CHORUS.

AND ALL HE SHOULD DO　　　　 AND ALL HE SHOULD DO
IS WRITE AND WRITE AND　　　 IS WRITE AND WRITE AND
　　WRITE　　　　　　　　　　　 　　WRITE
　　　　　　　　　　　　　　　　　 HIS WORDS SHOULD FLASH
　　　　　　　　　　　　　　　　　 OR HE GETS NO FOOD.
　　　　　　　　　　　　　　　　　 AND THIS SHOULD BE
AND THIS HIS ATTITUDE.　　　 HIS CUSTOMARY ATTITUDE.

CURTAIN

53

ACT TWO

It is moonlight.

Corcoran, leaning on column down left, is on the balcony. Louhedda is seated on stage left, gazing at him fondly.

CORCORAN.

    FAIR MOON, I'LL ASK UNTIL

        UPON MY GRAVE THEY PILE STONES:

    WHY WASN'T I NAMED DEMILLE,

        OR MAMOULIAN OR LEWIS MILESTONES?

    BORN 'NEATH A SMILING STAR,

        GAYEST OF SYBARITES,

        THEIR PICTURES ALWAYS ARE

        WELCOMED WITH JOY BY THE CRITICS.

    FOR ME THE STARS EXERT NO SPELL,

        I AM A SOUL FOR ALL TO PITY:

    MY LATEST FILM, 'TIS SAD TO TELL,

        HAS CLOSED AT RADIO CITY.

        FAIR MOON, I'LL ASK UNTIL

            UPON MY GRAVE THEY PILE STONES:

        WHY WASN'T I BORN DEMILLE,

            OR MAMOULIAN OR LEWIS MILESTONES?

        FAIR MOON, I'LL ASK UNTIL

            UPON MY GRAVE THEY PILE STONES.

LOUHEDDA.   How sweetly he carols forth his melody.... Good Mike, why are you sad? *(Corcoran comes D. from the balcony. Louhedda follows.)*

CORCORAN.   *(Faces her.)* My daughter is partial to a writer! A *writer!*

LOUHEDDA.   *(Concealing her emotions on this point.)* I have been so told.

CORCORAN.   *(Walks D.R. and back.)* Joe Porter suspects, though he does not know all. If she refuses to wed with him — if I cannot persuade her....

LOUHEDDA.   Yes? What then?

CORCORAN.   He will assign another to direct Poe's "The Raven" — those wonderful scenes! The stampede of the elephants, the temptation of Eve — The Jeffries-Johnson fight! Louhedda Butter-Up, if ever I was in need of butter it is now.

LOUHEDDA.   Perhaps it were unmaidenly that I should say it, but there *is* a way, good Mike … a way that would erase those darkling shadows. (*She draws a hand across his brow.*)

CORCORAN.   Tell me!

LOUHEDDA.   (*Archly — goes a few steps to L.*) If you and I — were to wed —

CORCORAN.   Wed!

LOUHEDDA.   (*Back to him.*) Be not hasty! Daily I would make mention of that greatest of directors, Mike Corcoran. Forget not — I am syndicated in 530 papers. Even the heart of Joe Porter would melt against that avalanche of mail. (*Corcoran looks at her appraisingly, trying to decide if she is worth it. Then his attention is drawn by a sound offstage.*)

HEBE.   (*Offstage L.*) Yes, Mr. Porter.

CORCORAN.   Hey, here comes Joe Porter.

LOUHEDDA.   (*As she leaves.*) Just think! I would have the exclusive story of the marriage! And if there is to be a baby, I would be the *first* to know it! (*Louhedda exits D.L. Joe Porter marches on with his Relatives, followed by Hebe, D.R.*)

PORTER.
> I AM THE MONARCH OF THE JOINT;
> ALL THAT I HAVE TO DO IS POINT.

You will notice that I've changed my pants.

HEBE.   An absolutely fascinating circumstance.

PORTER.   Let there be more light. (*Lights come up at once.*)

A RELATIVE.   (*Strain.*) Mr. Porter, how late do we have to work? We're all ready for the party.

ANOTHER RELATIVE. Yes, what about the party?

PORTER. The party will have to wait — I've got other troubles.

RELATIVE. Oh dear.

PORTER. I'm a very unhappy man.

HEBE. Mr. Porter is unhappy.

RELATIVES. Awww.

HEBE. Would you like them to sing for you, Mr. Porter?

PORTER. No, I don't think so.

HEBE. What about juggling? Would you like them to juggle?

PORTER. Yes, I'd like that.

HEBE. Do any of you girls juggle?

RELATIVES. Noooo we don't.

HEBE. They don't juggle.

PORTER. Do they know any card tricks?

HEBE. Do you know any card tricks?

RELATIVES. Noooo.

PORTER. Can they swim?

HEBE. Can you swim?

RELATIVES. Noooo.

PORTER. Can't swim, don't know any card tricks, can't juggle. What the hell are they doing in Hollywood?

RELATIVES. We want to marry Clark Gable.

RELATIVE. Yes. That's what we want.

HEBE. They want to marry Clark Gable.

PORTER. Oh.

HEBE. That's funny — so do I.

PORTER. What has Clark Gable got that I haven't got and where can I get it.

HEBE. It's a long story.

CORCORAN. Look, Joe, I've just been talking to Brenda. It seems the whole thing is a misunderstanding.

PORTER. No it isn't. I just went to see Brenda in her dressing room. She had a big picture of me up on the wall, and she was looking at it and she didn't know I was there. She looked right at the picture and she said, "Naaaaa" like that.

CORCORAN. She was just clearing her throat, Joe.

PORTER. You know Mike, I did a lot for Brenda. It's no easy thing for a girl to get into pictures. Brenda better be careful. I can discover another star just like that. I can take a little girl out of a little town and make her the biggest star in the country with the Academy Award and everything — a girl right out of a little town — I'll show you. *(Ballet. Bob and Sylvia Sin enter from D.L.)*

BOB. *(Crossing with Sylvia.)* You see, it's this way. First you get your picture in the movie magazines!

SYLVIA. The movie magazines!

BOB. Then it gets printed in *Look!*

SYLVIA. In *Look!*

BOB. And then finally you get on the cover of *Life!*

SYLVIA. *Life!* That'll be wonderful!

BOB. Sure! You'll do fine as long as you don't make a movie. *(They exit. D.R. Enter Louhedda through door U.R.)*

PORTER. But why don't you tell me what the secret is? That's what a secret is for — to tell!

LOUHEDDA. Well! But if you would consent to put Brenda Blossom out of your heart —

PORTER. Oh, so that's it — Why doesn't Brenda want to marry me? I'm not so terrible.

LOUHEDDA. *(Evasively.)* I know not the reason.

PORTER. She hasn't met Van Johnson?

LOUHEDDA. No!

PORTER. Every time I get so far with a girl, she meets Van Johnson.

LOUHEDDA. Joe, will you say unto Mike Corcoran that he may direct Poe's "The Raven?"

PORTER. Not unless you tell me the secret.

LOUHEDDA. I will give you a hint.

PORTER. *(Follows R.)* Good! What is it? Mineral, vegetable, animal or personal?

LOUHEDDA. It's just that sometimes you count on certain things being true, and they aren't.

PORTER. *(Turning.)* Certain things are true ... and they aren't true.

LOUHEDDA. Yes.

PORTER. That's a tough one.

LOUHEDDA. Other things are true instead.

PORTER. *(Mulling this one over.)* Other things are true instead. I may be dumb, but I still don't get it.

LOUHEDDA.

> HOLLYWOOD'S A FUNNY PLACE
> BIG STARS LITTLE STARLETS CHASE
> LITTLE GIRL ERMINE WRAPS
> TILL A MULTITUDE OF LAPS.

PORTER.

> VERY TRUE.
> SO THEY DO.

LOUHEDDA.

> SOMEHOW ALL THE WEEKLY CHECKS
> DEFINITELY HINGE ON SEX
> ONE MAN FILLS ANOTHER'S SHOES
> HARD TO TELL WHOSE BABY'S WHOSE.

PORTER.

> SO THEY BE,
> FREQUENTLEE.

LOUHEDDA.

> MANY AUTOGRAPHS ANNOY
> ELLA RAINES AND MYRNA LOY.
> GOLDWYN CLAIMS THAT ALL OUR ILLS
> CAN BE TRACED TO DOUBLE BILLS.

PORTER.

> YES, I KNOW.
> THAT IS SO.

> THOUGH TO GET YOUR DRIFT I'M STRIVING.
> IT IS SHADY, IT IS SHADY;
> I DON'T SEE AT WHAT YOU'RE DRIVING;
> MYSTIC LADY, MYSTIC LADY.

STERN CONVICTION'S O'ER ME PLAYING
THAT THERE IS NO MEANS OF WEIGHING
WHAT THE HELL THE LADY'S SAYING.

LOUHEDDA.

YES, I KNOW.
THAT IS SO.

PORTER.

THOUGH I'M ANYTHING BUT CLEVER,
I COULD TALK LIKE THIS FOREVER;
FILMS ABOUT A CHINESE SLEUTH
PLAY TO MILLIONS IN DULUTH.

LOUHEDDA.

VERY TRUE.
SO THEY DO.

PORTER.

MANY THOUSANDS ARE EMPLOYED
SPOILING NICE CLEAN CELLULOID.
PLOTS THAT SHOULDN'T REACH REHEARSAL
DRAW IN DOUGH FOR UNIVERSAL.

LOUHEDDA.

FREQUENTLEE
I AGREE.

PORTER.

IN GRASS SKIRTS YOU SEE THE CLEAR KNEE,
SOMETIMES MORE, OF MISS GENE TIERNEY.
GRABLE'S SHORTS ARE NICE AND LACY,
NOT SO THOSE OF SPENCER TRACY.

LOUHEDDA.

YES I KNOW.
THAT IS SO.

> THOUGH TO CATCH MY DRIFT HE'S STRIVING,
>> I'LL DISSEMBLE, I'LL DISSEMBLE;
> WHEN HE SEES AT WHAT I'M DRIVING,
>> LET HIM TREMBLE, LET HIM TREMBLE.

LOUHEDDA and PORTER.
> THOUGH A MYSTIC TONE I BORROW,
> HE WILL LEARN THE TRUTH WITH SORROW;
> HERE TODAY AND GONE TOMORROW.

PORTER.
> AIN'T IT SO.

LOUHEDDA.
> I DON'T KNOW.

PORTER.	LOUHEDDA.
THOUGH A MYSTIC TONE I BORROW	I'LL DISSEMBLE, I'LL DISSEMBLE,
I WILL LEARN THE TRUTH WITH SORROW;	LET HIM TREMBLE,
HERE TODAY AND GONE TOMORROW.	LET HIM TREMBLE,
	LET HIM TREMBLE,
	THERE'S YOUR HINT.

PORTER.
> NO IT AIN'T!

Say, wait a minute, you didn't tell me the secret — *(Porter and Louhedda exit D.L. Brenda comes in — walking slowly, thoughtfully. Dick Live-eye enters, U.C. with red patch, all alertness.)*

DICK.   Pssst!

BRENDA.   Mr. Live-eye.

DICK.   I would have speech with you.

BRENDA.   Speech with me?

DICK. Speech with you. I shall have most of the speeches, but it will be with *you*. Tell me — have you an agent?

BRENDA. *(She nods.)* The firm of Drawingbord and Smorgasbord.

DICK. Smorgasbord is a good man. But I am a better.

BRENDA. Alas, I have a long contract.

DICK. How long?

BRENDA. 85 years — with options.

DICK. Smorgasbord is a *very* good man. *(Aside walking D.R.)* I must persuade her to break the contract. I must frighten her. *(Aloud, to Brenda, pacing towards her.)* Know you the plan that Mr. Porter has prepared for you, providing you yield not to his entreaties?

BRENDA. Plan? What, pray?

DICK. You will never be heard of again! He will doom you to a life of obscurity!

BRENDA. *(Steps back.)* You affright me! He will exile me to some distant rock?

DICK. Worse! No human eye will ever behold you! He will put you upon the *stage!*

BRENDA. *(Recoiling a step.)* The stage!

DICK. Know you that upon the stage some actresses receive as little as a thousand dollars a week?

BRENDA. *(Steps back.)* It cannot be!

DICK. *(Advancing L.)* 'Tis true! Know you that a stage actress, upon arrival in New York City, is met by no press agent, no American Beauty roses, and sometimes by no more than a crowd of two-hundred people! It's a living death.

BRENDA. Oh, pity me.

DICK. No photographs in the nightclubs, no pictures in stage magazines —

there *are* no stage magazines!

BRENDA.   He could not inflict such torture!

DICK.   *(Goes D.R. then turns.)* But he will! And one thing more — one last in-dignity! On the stage you have to *act!*

BRENDA.   No, no! *(Goes on her knees, clasps hands.)*

DICK.   *(Down to her.)* And should you give a bad performance upon the stage, the critics actually *say so* — in print!

BRENDA.   Alack-a-day! No!

DICK.   Yes! All this if you do not wed with Joe Porter!

BRENDA.   Alas! What can I do?

DICK.   *(Leaning close to her — crosses D.L.)* Think! Think! What would Smorgasbord do? *(Aside to audience.)* Methinks I've scared the hell out of her! *(Exits D.L.)*

BRENDA.   *(As Dick exits.)*

> TO GO UPON THE STAGE!
>> A PROSPECT MOST DISTRACTING!
> TO THEREUPON ENGAGE
>> IN PLAIN AND SIMPLE ACTING!
> GREAT IS MY LOVE, BUT ALSO MY AMBITION;
>> PERHAPS I SHOULD CONSIDER MY POSITION:
> ON THE ONE HAND, THE GOLD-AND-SILVER SCREEN,
>> A LIFE OF MOST ATTRACTIVE EASE AND PLENTY —
> LEST THERE BE ANY DOUBT OF WHAT I MEAN:
>> ABOUT A MILLION BUCKS BEFORE I'M TWENTY.
> A LIFE THAT I AM NOW EMBEDDED FIRM IN,
>> WITH GORGEOUS COATS OF SABLE, MINK, AND ERMINE.
>
> ON THE OTHER HAND, A DARK AND DINGY ROOM,
>> IN SOME BACK STREET WITH STUFFY CHILDREN CRYING,

WHERE ORGANS YELL, AND CLACKING HOUSEWIVES FUME,
    AND CLOTHES ARE HANGING OUT ALL DAY A-DRYING.
WITH NO PROJECTION ROOM TO KEEP TIME SPEEDING,
    BUT JUST A LOT OF PRINTED BOOKS FOR READING.

A WRITER HELD 'NEATH KEY AND LOCK,
    WHOSE SOUL IS NOT HIS OWN,
WHO TOILS FOR BREAD FROM NINE O'CLOCK
    TILL HALF THE NIGHT HAS FLOWN.
    TILL HALF THE NIGHT HAS FLOWN.
NO GOLDEN RANK CAN BE IMPART,
    NO CROESUS HE OF MEN,
NO FORTUNE SAVE HIS TRUSTY HEART,
    AND DOLLAR FOUNTAIN PEN.
    HIS TRUSTY HEART AND FOUNTAIN PEN.
AND YET HE IS SO WONDROUS FAIR
    THAT LOVE FOR ONE SO PASSING RARE,
    SO PEERLESS IN HIS MANLY BEAUTY,
    WERE LITTLE ELSE THAN SOLEMN DUTY,
    WERE LITTLE ELSE THAN SOLEMN DUTY.

OH, GOD OF LOVE, AND GOD OF REASON, SAY
    WHICH OF YOU TWAIN SHALL MY POOR HEART OBEY?

A WRITER HELD 'NEATH KEY AND LOCK
    WHOSE SOUL IS NOT HIS OWN
NO GOLDEN RANK CAN HE IMPART
    NO CROESUS HE OF MEN,
NO FORTUNE SAVE HIS TRUSTY HEART AND DOLLAR
        FOUNTAIN PEN
    HIS TRUSTY HEART AND FOUNTAIN PEN.

GOD OF LOVE, GOD OF REASON,
    GOD OF REASON, GOD OF LOVE,
    SAY WHICH SHALL MY POOR HEART OBEY
OH GOD OF LOVE AND GOD OF REASON

SAY, OH GOD OF LOVE AND GOD OF REASON,
SAY WHICH OF YOU TWAIN SHALL MY POOR HEART OBEY,
MY HEART OBEY
WHICH SHALL MY HEART, MY HEART OBEY.

(Miss Hebe enters U.R. claps her hands sharply. At once two Pages dance each side D.L. with six chairs and conference table. At the same time enter Dick U.C.L., Bob D.L., Corcoran U.L.C., and Ralph D.L. All this to music.)

DICK.   *(Entering from U.C.L.)* I just want to be the agent for John D. Rockefeller — that's all I ask.

BOB.   *(Entering from D.L.)* So I said to Selznick, "You can't talk like that to me!" and he said, "I can't, can't I?" and I said, "No, you can't." So he did. *(They stand around conference table which has just been brought in from R. by two other Pages.)*

PORTER.   *(Enters from D.R.)* Going to have a poker game.

HEBE.   It's time for the conference, Mr. Porter.

PORTER.   What conference?

HEBE.   The story conference. To decide what pictures to make.

PORTER.   *All right* — the meeting will come to order. *(They quiet down. Hebe produces telephone.)* Hello. Don't ring me unless somebody's on the phone.... Isn't it time for my graham crackers and milk.

HEBE.   Coming up! *(Hebe produces bowl, crackers, milk, spoon. Porter becomes completely absorbed in eating.)*

PORTER.   What are you fellows doing here?

HEBE.   The conference Mr. Porter!

PORTER.   Oh yes, we're going to plan the pictures for next year. Is that right?

HEBE and OTHERS.   Yes, Mr. Porter. — Yes, that's right. — Yes.

PORTER.   This is a whole new idea. Planning the pictures.

DICK.   I'll tell you what I think. I think that Pinafore ought to make a prestige picture.

CORCORAN.   That's a good idea!

BOB.   Yes!

PORTER.   Make what?

DICK.   A prestige picture.

PORTER.   What's that?

DICK.   A prestige picture is a picture that loses money, but it gives you prestige. Then with the prestige you sell your stinkers and get the money back.

PORTER.   That leaves you just where you were in the first place.

DICK.   That's right.

PORTER.   Then what's the use of doing it?

DICK.   Because everybody else does it.

PORTER.   Oh! If everybody else does it, we've got to do it too … All those in favor of making a prestige picture, say aye.

DICK.   Aye!

CORCORAN.   Aye!

BOB.   Aye!

RALPH.   Aye!

PORTER.   *(Pointing to Ralph.)* Who's that?

BOB.   That's the writer, Mr. Porter. He's going to write the picture.

PORTER.   Oh! Well, *he* shouldn't have anything to say.

BOB.   No, sir. *(Others agree.)*

PORTER. Don't we usually tie 'em up at the conference?

BOB. Yes, sir. I forgot. *(He rises and ties a gag around Ralph's mouth.)*

PORTER. Now where were we?

DICK. We want to make a picture that'll lose money.

PORTER. That's pretty hard to do.

DICK. H'm. What about a remake of *Parnell?*

CORCORAN. Times have changed — they go to anything now.

DICK. Yeah.

BOB. Yup.

PORTER. I know what! *(Phone.)* Get me the New York office.... We'll buy a play — a play off the stage. You can generally lose money on those.

CORCORAN. That's a good idea. *(Vague noises come from Ralph.)*

PORTER. What's the matter with *him?*

BOB. He's trying to say something.

PORTER. He heard us talking. Fix it so he can't hear.

BOB. I'm sorry, sir. *(He arranges a bandanna around Ralph's ears.)*

PORTER. *(Phone.)* Hello!... Here's New York ... Jack? This is Joe.... What's the name of that play that's running in New York? About a guy that never gets there on time — What? *The Late Mr. Appulee.* Well, we want to buy the motion picture rights. Find out how much they want for it.... How much. A hundred-and-fifty-thousand dollars?

DICK. No, no!

CORCORAN. That'll never do!

DICK. Will they take five-hundred-thousand?

PORTER. *(Phone.)* Find out if they'll take five-hundred-thousand.... What?... Two-hundred-thousand is the most.

DICK. Hang up!

PORTER. Never mind, Jack. Thanks a lot. *(He hangs up.)*

CORCORAN. You couldn't lose anything that way.

OTHERS. No, no.

PORTER. No, looks as though we're kind of stuck.

DICK. Yah.

OTHERS. Yah, yah. *(Pause.)*

PORTER. What happens if a prestige picture *makes* money?

DICK. Oh, you can't do that.

OTHERS. No, no.

PORTER. I just wondered.

CORCORAN. Now look — a prestige picture has got to be *about* somebody. You know, like that picture *Wilson.*

PORTER. Who was that about?

CORCORAN. That was about Wilson.

PORTER. Oh, then we can't do him again. It's too soon.

BOB. There must be somebody else.

DICK. Let's see ... Lincoln, Pasteur, Disraeli, Nora Bayes....

CORCORAN. All of the well-known ones have been done. They're *too* well-known.

PORTER. *(Nods.)* We need a well-known man that nobody has ever heard of.

OTHERS. Yah, yah. *(More mumbles from Ralph.)*

PORTER. He's still trying to talk.

BOB. I'll tie it tighter. *(He does so.)*

PORTER. He can still see. *(Bob ties another kerchief around Ralph's eyes.)*

CORCORAN. How about a man like Thoreau? A famous naturalist?

PORTER. What's a naturalist?

CORCORAN. A naturalist is a man that behaves naturally.

PORTER. The Hays office wouldn't stand for that.

OTHERS. No, no.

DICK. If I could just think of the right character.

RALPH. *(Bursting his bonds — rises. Corcoran and Bob restrain him.)* I know: Make a picture about Mr. Porter!

PORTER. *(Rises — also Hebe, Bob.)* Say!

DICK. *(Rises.)* That's right, Portie! *You*'re well-known and nobody's ever heard of you!

PORTER. Good for you! What's your salary?

RALPH. 80 dollars a week, sir.

PORTER. From now on it's 85. Oh, boy! What a picture! *The Life of Joe Porter, or From Rags to Rushes,* in technique color.

DICK. I'll cast it!

CORCORAN. I'll direct it!

BOB.   I'll advertise it!

HEBE.   I'll skip it!

DICK.   It'll be the greatest picture ever produced! You know why? *(All sit.)*

PORTER.

YES, I KNOW WHY, CAUSE YOU GET TEN PERCENT.

DICK.

HE IS A MOVIE MAN.

PORTER.

I AM A MOVIE MAN.

DICK.

FROM THE HOUSETOPS LET US CRY IT:
THAT HE IS A MOVIE MAN! HE'S THE LAST MAN TO DENY IT!

ALL but PORTER.

THAT HE IS A MOVIE MAN!

DICK.

MIGHT HAVE BEEN A BAREBACK RIDER.

PORTER.

ON A HORSE OR SOMETHING WIDER,

DICK.

OR CHEF WITH FRYING PAN.

ALL but PORTER.

OR CHEF WITH FRYING PAN.

DICK.

BUT IN SPITE OF ALL TEMPTATIONS
TOWARD OTHER OCCUPATIONS,
HE REMAINS A MOVIE MAN!

(All rise as table and chairs are cleared.)

ALL but PORTER.

   HE RE-MAI-AI-AI-AI-AI-AI-AI-NS A MOVIE MAN!

PORTER.

   HE RE-MAI-AI-AI-AI-AI-AI-AI-NS A MOVIE MAN!

DICK.

   OH, OH.... NOT AGAIN.... PLEASE.

Portie, I've got a little bad news for you.

PORTER.   Why don't you mail it, and then my secretary will open it and maybe she won't show it to me.

DICK.   It's about Poe's "The Raven."

PORTER.   Poe's "The Raven?"

DICK.   Yeah.

PORTER.   What about it?

DICK.   It seems you haven't got the rights after all. Darryl Zanuck has got it!

PORTER.   Zanuck! He's another one. Everything I want, either Van Johnson gets it, or Darryl Zanuck.... How do you know he's got it?

DICK.   I just got a telegram.

PORTER.   Who from?

DICK.   From Edgar Allen Poe.

PORTER.   Poe! What do you know.

DICK.   What's the difference. You don't have to worry, though — I've just had a great idea. Why don't you buy Poe's "The Stork?"

PORTER.   Poe's Stork. What's that about?

DICK. What do you think it's about. A stork. "The Raven" is about a raven isn't it?

PORTER. I guess so.

DICK. Guess so? You've read it, haven't you?

PORTER. Well, I've read a two-page synopsis. *(He struggles to recall a little.)* Said the Raven, "Never again."

DICK. That's it! Only instead of "Never again" with the stork it's just once more.

PORTER. I get it! That's the only difference?

DICK. That's the only difference.

PORTER. I'll buy it!

DICK. *(Suddenly remembering.)* I completely forgot!

PORTER. What?

DICK. Zanuck has got "The Stork," too. — Going to make a double feature.

PORTER. Zanuck! Zanuck! I'm getting tired of Zanuck! *(He calls.)* Somebody come here!... I'll fix him! *(Miss Hebe enters D.R. Porter crosses R. to her.)*

HEBE. Yes, Mr. Porter.

PORTER. I want you to put up a studio order! The name Darryl Zanuck is never to be mentioned by anybody at the Pinafore studio. Whoever mentions him gets fired! Tell everybody!

HEBE. Yes, Mr. Porter.

PORTER. And that goes for Van Johnson, too!

HEBE. Yes, Mr. Porter. *(Hebe exits.)*

PORTER. Darryl Zanuck, Van Johnson, Van Johnson, Darryl Zanuck — that finishes *them!*

DICK. *(Slyly.)* Well, now that you haven't got a picture for her, there's no use keeping Brenda Blossom on salary, is there?

PORTER. I was sort of thinking of marrying her. She wouldn't get any salary then.

DICK. That's so. The only trouble is ... I don't know whether I ought to say this....

PORTER. Is what? Everybody's mysterious around here. Are *you* going to be mysterious too?

DICK. Me? No-o-o-o! *(Sings.)*
    JOE PORTER, I'VE IMPORTANT INFORMATION,
        SING HEY, THE KINDLY BOSS OF ALL WHO WORK,
    ABOUT A CERTAIN INTIMATE RELATION,
        SING HEY, THE MERRY MAIDEN AND THE JERK,

PORTER and DICK.
    THE MERRY MAIDEN
    THE MERRY MAIDEN
    THE MAIDEN AND THE JERK.

PORTER.
    DICK LIVE-EYE, YOU CAN TAKE YOUR INFORMATION,
        SING HEY, THE TEN-PER-CENTER THAT YOU ARE,
    AND PUT IT WITH YOUR FONDEST ASPIRATION,
        SING HEY, FUNICULI, FUNICULAR!

PORTER and DICK.
    SING HEY, FUNICULI,
    SING HEY FUNICULA, FUNICULI, FUNICULAR!

DICK.
    IF *YOU* HIDE ON THE BALCONY AND GLANCE DOWN,
        SING HEY, SING NONNIE AND SLACK-A-DAY,
    YOU'LL FIND THEY'RE GOING TO CATCH YOU WITH YOUR

> PANTS DOWN,
>> SING HEY, YOU WON'T LOOK VERY GOOD THAT WAY.

PORTER and DICK.
> I WON'T LOOK VERY GOOD, I WON'T LOOK VERY GOOD,
>> SING HEY, I WON'T LOOK VERY GOOD THAT WAY.

PORTER.
> I DON'T KNOW WHAT IT IS THAT YOU WANT FIXED UP,
>> SING HEY, IT ALL KEEPS RINGING IN MY HEAD,
> IT'S ALL SO ABRACADABRA AND MIXED UP,
>> SING HEY, I THINK I'D LIKE TO GO TO BED.

PORTER and DICK.
> I THINK I'D LIKE TO GO TO BED
> I THINK I'D LIKE TO GO TO BED
>> SING HEY, HE THINKS HE'D LIKE TO GO TO BED.

DICK.
> JOE PORTER, YOUR YOUNG LADY IS A -SIGHING,
>> SING HEY, AND YOU CAN PASTE THIS IN YOUR HAT,
> THIS VERY NIGHT WITH RACKSTRAW TO BE FLYING,
>> SING HEY, WHAT HAVE YOU GO TO SAY TO *THAT*?

PORTER and DICK.
> WHAT HAVE I GOT TO SAY TO THAT?
> WHAT HAVE I GOT TO SAY TO THAT?
>> SING HEY, WHAT HAVE YOU GOT TO SAY TO THAT?

PORTER.
> DICK LIVE-EYE, I WILL HIDE UP IN THE GALL'RY,
>> SING HEY, IF WHAT YOU'RE TELLING ME IS SOUND,
> I'LL TAKE AWAY THE LOUSE'S RAISE IN SAL'RY,
>> SING HEY, FOR I'M THE TOUGHEST GUY AROUND.

PORTER and DICK.
> FOR I'M THE TOUGHEST GUY AROUND

FOR I'M THE TOUGHEST GUY AROUND

SING HEY, FOR HE'S THE TOUGHEST GUY AROUND.

PORTER.   *(As the music stops.)* Let there be no light! *(Blackout. Brenda enters D.L., and a small spot is thrown on her.)*

BRENDA.   I will hesitate no longer, 'tis Ralph I love, and naught else matters. We shall away this night to Yuma, and be wed. *(The light goes out. Now a similar spot is thrown on Corcoran, on the D.R. side of the stage. He is dressed in something out of about the 8th century, something with a great cloak, behind which he can conceal himself.)*

CORCORAN.   In this costume out of wardrobe they will know me not. I must stop her flight, if I am to direct Poe's "The Raven." *(Spot on Dick on L. balcony.)*

DICK.   Be not surprised which side you find *me* on. I am but here to mess things up. *(Exits B.L. Now the lights on Porter on R. balcony.)*

PORTER.   All *I* know is that somehow I'm going to get the worst of it. *(The spotlight goes out.)* Let there be moonlight! *(The room is immediately bathed in moon-light. He exits B.R. Brenda and a group of Girls tiptoe in from L. side; Ralph and a group of Writers tiptoe in from the R.)*

ALL.

> CAREFULLY ON TIPTOE STEALING
> > BREATHING GENTLY AS WE MAY
> EV'RY STEP WITH CAUTION FEELING.
> > WE WILL SOFTLY STEAL AWAY.
> > GOODNESS ME!
> WHAT DID WE STRIKE?

DICK.

> SILENT BE!
> > IT WAS THE MIKE!

ALL.   *(Reassured.)*

> IT WAS — IT WAS THE MIKE.

75

CORCORAN.

    THEY'RE RIGHT — IT WAS THE MIKE!

ALL.

    THEY ARE OFF, THEY'RE OFF TO YUMA —
        BEARD THE CLERGY IN HIS LAIR,
    NEITHER HORSES WILD NOR PUMA
        CAN RESTRAIN THIS HAPPY PAIR.
    GOODNESS ME,
    WHAT DID WE STRIKE?

DICK.

    SILENT BE!
    AGAIN THE MIKE!

ALL.

    IT WAS AGAIN THE MIKE!

CORCORAN.

    THEY'RE RIGHT — IT WAS THE MIKE.

(Lights come on full.)

    PRETTY DAUGHTER OF MINE,
        I INSIST UPON KNOWING
        WHERE YOU MAY BE GOING
    WITH MEN OF SUCH DESIGN.
    THIS EVIL-SMELLING CREW,
        RACKSTRAW AND MCCAFFERY,
        THEY'RE FAR TOO RIFF-RAFFERY,
    MY DAUGHTER, FOR YOU.

WRITERS.

    NOW HARK AT THAT, DO
        RACKSTRAW AND MCCAFFERY
        ARE TOO RIFF-RAFFERY,
    FOR A LADY LIKE YOU!

RALPH.

> PROUD CORCORAN, THAT HAUGHTY LIP UNCURL!
>
> VAIN MAN, SUPPRESS THAT SUPERCILIOUS SNEER!
>
> FOR I HAVE DARED TO LOVE YOUR MATCHLESS GIRL!
>
> JUST PUT A BIT OF *THAT*, SIR, IN YOUR BEER!

CORCORAN.

> YOUR PETTY CLAIMS DO NOT CONCERN HER —
>
> THINK TO WHOM YOU ASPIRE!
>
> A STAR WHO'S UP WITH LANA TURNER
>
> AND I HER FAMOUS SIRE,
>
> REMEMBER I'M A BIG DIRECTOR,
>
> WHO CALLS VAN JOHNSON VAN,
>
> OF MOVIE NAMES A GREAT RESPECTER,
>
> AND WHO CALLS ZANUCK ZAN!

ALL.

> OH!

CORCORAN.

> WHO CALLS VAN JOHNSON VAN!

ALL.

> OH!

CORCORAN.

> AND WHO CALLS ZANUCK ZAN!

HEBE.   *(Enters U.L.)*

> DID YOU HEAR HIM, DID YOU HEAR HIM?
>
> HE HAS THROWN US ALL IN PANIC!
>
> DON'T GO NEAR HIM, DON'T GO NEAR HIM!
>
> HE SAID JOHNSON, HE SAID ZANUCK!

(Every eye goes to the balcony, where Porter now emerges from behind a door. With slow and portentous steps he comes down the stairs and advances upon Corcoran.)

PORTER.

> THIS PAINFUL EPISODE

GIVES YOU A CHANCE TO SEE A MAN EXPLODE;
THE EXTENT OF YOUR DISGRACE
YOU MAY LEARN FROM THE EXPRESSION ON MY FACE.

(He puts on a fierce expression.)

CORCORAN.
    AM I THEN AT THE FINISH OF MY TETHER?
        REFLECT, PRAY, ON WHAT SUCH A VERDICT MEANS;
    REMEMBER, WE'VE PLAYED PINOCHLE TOGETHER;
        FOR YOU I ONCE DID NOT MELD SIXTY QUEENS!

PORTER.
    YOU CANNOT FOR THIS CRIME ACCOUNT!
        NO ONE CAN SUCH A SIN AFFORD,
    SO, GET YE HENCE TO PARAMOUNT —
        BE ANYTHING BUT PINAFORED
    TO METRO OR TO WARNERS GO!
        BE FREELANCE AND ADVENTURY!
    OR SEEK REPUBLIC, R-K-O,
        OR FOX TWENTIETH-CENTURY!

(Dick enters D.L.)

ALL.
    OR SEEK REPUBLIC, R-K-O,
    OR FOX TWENTIETH CENTURY!

PORTER.   Well?

CORCORAN.   I must find a good agent. *(He goes.)*

DICK.   What did he say? Hey! Before you sign with Feldman. Hey! *(Follows him D.R.)*

PORTER.   *(Advancing on the female relatives.)*
    NOW, WOULD ANY OF YOU DAMES

CARE TO MENTION THOSE TWO NAMES?
BECAUSE IF YOU WANT TO, HERE'S A DAMN GOOD CHANCE!

HEBE.
NO, NO! NOT YOUR SISTERS AND YOUR COUSINS AND
YOUR AUNTS.

PORTER.   *That's* settled! Now let's see what goes on here. *(He singles out Ralph.)* Hey you with the hat band, come forward, my fine-feathered friend!   I would fain pluck a few feathers.

RALPH.   I am proud to step forward, sir, and proud to avow my love for this fairest bud that ever blossomed.

BRENDA.   *(Rushing to Ralph's arms.)* Darling!

PORTER.   *(Breaking them apart.)* All right, all right — now that's over.... What's your name again?

RALPH.   Ralph Rackstraw, sir.

PORTER.   Rafe? How do you spell it?

RALPH.   R-a-l-p-h, sir.

PORTER.   R-a-l-p-h, Rafe?

RALPH.   Yes, sir.

PORTER.   I'm going to put you some place where you'll be s-a-l-p-h, *safe.*

BRENDA.   Oh, spare him, for I love him tenderly! Please, Uncle Joe!

PORTER.   Uncle Joe? That settles it! Seize him! *(Ralph is seized by Bob who has rushed in D.R.)* Have we such a thing as a doghouse in the studio? *(Louhedda enters U.L.)*

BOB.   We have!

PORTER.   Then load him with chains and take him there at once! *(Crosses to L. of Brenda — she goes to L. of Ralph.)* You can sing one more number.

RALPH.
> FAREWELL MY OWN,
>> LIGHT OF MY LIFE, FAREWELL.

BRENDA.
> AND ALL ALONE
>> REJOICE IN YOUR DOGHOUSE CELL!

PORTER.
> LET HIM BE SHOWN
>> AT ONCE TO HIS DOGHOUSE CELL!
> TOSS HIM A BONE,
>> AND MAYBE A PEANUT SHELL!

LOUHEDDA.   *(On balcony U.L.)*
> BUT WHEN IS KNOWN THE SECRET I HAVE TO TELL
> WIDE, WILL BE THROWN THE DOOR OF HIS DOGHOUSE CELL!

BRENDA, HEBE, PORTER,
LOUHEDDA and BOB.   CHORUS.

FAREWELL, MY OWN, LIGHT	HE'LL HEAR NO TONE OF HER
OF MY LIFE FAREWELL	HE LOVES SO WELL,
AND ALL ALONE REJOICE IN	FOR CRIME UNKNOWN
YOUR DOGHOUSE	HE GOES TO A DOGHOUSE
YOUR DOGHOUSE CELL.	A DOGHOUSE CELL.

(Ralph is led out D.R. by Bob, who reenters immediately. Brenda exits D.L. Louhedda exits U.C. Porter goes to D.C.R. approvingly.)

PORTER.
> WHEN YOU GOTTA GO, YOU GOT TO GO —
> IS AN OLD-ESTABLISHED CUSTOM OF THE STUDIO.

ALL.

WHEN YOU GOTTA GO, YOU GOT TO GO —
IS AN OLD-ESTABLISHED CUSTOM OF THE STUDIO.

(Bob enters D.R. — shakes Porter's hand, crosses to L. Hebe in the middle, Porter on R. Louhedda is now C.R., Dick returns D.R. rubbing his hands in satisfaction and stands to her right.)

DICK.   *(To Louhedda.)* I signed him! How's that for a night's work? Porter has lost Poe's "The Raven," Brenda has lost Ralph Rackstraw, Rackstraw is in the doghouse — *(Crosses D.L.)*

LOUHEDDA.   ... Tell me, Dick Live-eye! Why do you do these things? What is your fell purpose?

DICK.   Purpose? Just messing things up! I'm an agent!

LOUHEDDA.   I will not have it. I will *tell!*

DICK.   Tell what?

LOUHEDDA.   Come, good people! *(Up to balcony.)* Come one, come all! Come! *(The all stream in, chattering — including Bob. Louhedda sings.)*

LOUHEDDA.
THE TOWN I NOW MUST SHAKE —
PRAY GIVE YOUR EAR!
A LONG-CONCEALED MISTAKE
I WOULD MAKE CLEAR.

(A buzz of talk. "Mistake!" "What means she?" "Never before has she acknowledged error!")

I OFTEN TIMES CONFUSE
THE WOOD THAT'S KNOWN AS HOLLY,
FOR WHEN IT COMES TO NEWS
I'M SLIGHTLY OFF MY TROLLEY.

ALL.

    NOW THIS IS FAR FROM JOLLY
    SHE'S SLIGHTLY OFF HER TROLLEY;
    THE WOOD THAT'S KNOWN AS HOLLY
        WILL SING THE MOVIE BLUES.

LOUHEDDA.

    IF I BE RIGHT OR WRONG
        IS PRETTY MUCH A TOSS-UP;
    YOU WHO HAVE KNOWN ME LONG
        TAKE SALT WITH ALL MY GOSSIP.

ALL.

    IT'S PRETTY MUCH A TOSS-UP;
    WE TAKE SALT WITH HER GOSS-UP;
    THEN ADD THE GAIN OR LOSS UP,
        AND SADLY SING OUR SONG.

LOUHEDDA.

    A CERTAIN MAN WAS HIRED
        TO FILL A LOW POSITION
    ANOTHER MUCH ADMIRED
        WAS GIVEN LOFTY MISSION.

ALL.

    ONE FILLED A LOW POSITION,
    AND ONE A HIGHER MISSION —
    A FRIENDLY COMPETITION,
        WITH GENIUS FIRED.

LOUHEDDA.

    NONE SO CONFUSED AS I;
        IN THAT I BOW TO NO ONE;
    I GAVE LOW JOB TO HIGH,
        AND HIGHER JOB TO LOW ONE.

ALL.

    IN THAT SHE BOWS TO KNOW ONE;
    SHE GAVE HIGH JOB TO LOW ONE;

THE GAL'S ENOUGH TO THROW ONE;
    OH ME, OH ME, OH MY.

LOUHEDDA.

    THIS THEN LOUHEDDA'S CROSS
        THAT RISES NOW TO SMITE HER;
    ONE OF THE TWAIN YOUR BOSS,
        THE OTHER ONE A WRITER.

ALL.

    ONE OF THE TWAIN A WRITER;
    IT RISES NOW TO SMITE HER;
    HER BRAIN THOUGH SOMEWHAT LIGHTER
        IS MADE OF SPANISH MOSS.

DICK.   But have I heard aright? He who now heads the studio was meant to be but a writer, whereas a writer should properly rule all?

LOUHEDDA.   Alas, 'tis true. The twain were appointed by the studio upon the same day. But in copying the news for my column I seem to have reversed the names. It was just a slight mistake.

DICK.   It's a good thing you're not handling the presidential elections.

BOB.   But who is our new boss? Who the writer thus shamefully deprived of power?

DICK.   Yes, who is he?

DOORMAN.   *(Entering D.R.)* Mr. Ralph Rackstraw, new head of the studio. Five million dollars a year! *(Bob steps back U. amazed and goes to L. desk. Enter Ralph, U.C, now in handsome cutaway, followed by Hebe and relatives.)*

CHORUS.

    THEN WE'LL BE YOUR SISTERS AND YOUR COUSINS AND
        YOUR AUNTS,
    YOUR SISTERS, AND YOUR COUSINS WHOM YOU RECKON UP
        BY DOZENS. AND YOUR AUNTS.

RALPH.

    I AM THE MONARCH OF THE PLACE;

    AND I ACCEPT THE JOB WITH GRACE;

    I HAVE NO EXPERIENCE WITH HIGH FINANCE —

HEBE. *(Rushing to him.)*

    THEN WE'LL BE YOUR SISTERS AND YOUR COUSINS AND
        YOUR AUNTS!

CHORUS.

    THEN WE'LL BE YOUR SISTERS AND YOUR COUSINS AND
        YOUR AUNTS,

    YOUR SISTERS, AND YOUR COUSINS WHOM YOU RECKON UP
        BY DOZENS.

    AND YOUR AUNTS.

DOORMAN.   Joe Porter, writer. 75 dollars a week! *(Enter Porter U.C. now in convict clothes.)*

PORTER.   I stepped from under the mistletoe, now I'm not the ruler of the studio. *(Chorus repeats. Brenda is heard singing off L. as she approaches. She enters U.L.)*

BRENDA.

    HERE ON THE LOT I AM A STAR —

(Enters D.L. and goes C. to Ralph.)

    WHAT HAVE I GOT THAT OTHERS LONG FOR?

    BEAUTIFUL HOUSE AND HANDSOME CAR,

    EVERYTHING *AND* THE LAD I'M STRONG FOR.

(Corcoran enters U.B.R. and goes C.)

CORCORAN.   Well, it's all settled. I'm going to start my own company — Mike Corcoran Productions.

LOUHEDDA.   Mike!

RALPH.   *(Goes D.C. with Brenda.)* No! For you will be my father-in-law, and in accordance with an old studio custom I now sign you for *twice* your old salary or 60 times what you are worth.

ALL.   Hooray!

RALPH.   Your first job is to direct Poe's "The Raven." *(Then he goes back U.C. with Brenda.)*

PORTER.   Poe's "The Raven," but Zanuck has got it!

DICK.   No, he hasn't! I just talked to Zanuck. He's going to do Poe's "Woodpecker."

CORCORAN.   *(Dreamily.)* Twice my salary, and half of it is yours under the community property law.

LOUHEDDA.   Mike darling, that's the sweetest cash proposal I've every had.

PORTER.   But wait! Everybody's getting married! Where does that leave me?

HEBE.   *(Crosses D.L. to his R. linking her arm with his.)* Even a writer needs a secretary.

PORTER.   That's right. So he does! To do his writing!

HEBE.   Yes, Joe.

PORTER.   We'll have a triple wedding, but separate honeymoons.

BOB.   Three loving pairs.

DICK.   — And I get ten percent.

FINALE

WE ARE SIMPLE MOVIE FOLK
OF THE WOOD THAT'S KNOWN AS HOLLY;
AND WE LIGHTLY BEAR THE YOKE
OF A LIFE OF LOVELY FOLLY.

SO, WE END AS WE BEGAN

WE SUBMIT THIS TRIFLING FILBERT

WITH APOLOGIES TO GILBERT

AND ALSO SULLIVAN

WITH APOLOGIES TO GILBERT AND SULLIVAN

WITH APOLOGIES TO GILBERT AND SULLIVAN.

END

PROPERTY LIST

Basket with folded newspapers (LOUHEDDA)
Pencil (LOUHEDDA)
Small notebook (LOUHEDDA)
Gold cigarette case (DICK)
Cigarettes (PAGES)
Money (PAGES)
Script (RALPH)
Megaphones with "PP" on them
Large portfolio (HEBE)
Hollywood Reporter newspaper (HEBE)
Gun (GUARD)
Eye patches (DICK)
Scripts (CORCORAN, GIRL, SYLVIA)
Books (GIRLS)
Cake (MAN 1)
Tray with head (MAN 2)
Leopard skin (HEBE)
Pail and mop (BEVERLY)
Bowl (HEBE)
Graham crackers (HEBE)
Milk (HEBE)
Spoon (HEBE)
Gag (BOB)
Bandanna (BOB)
Kerchief (BOB)

SOUND EFFECTS

Telephone ring